THE PONCA CHIEFS

THE PONCA
CHIEFS

An Account of the Trial of Standing Bear

Thomas Henry Tibbles

Edited with an introduction
by Kay Graber

UNIVERSITY OF NEBRASKA PRESS • LINCOLN

Manufactured in the United States of America

Contents

Editor's Introduction

In 1969 a group of American Indians landed on Alcatraz Island and claimed possession of it under the terms of an old treaty providing that certain abandoned federal property would revert to the tribe. As television cameras and newspapermen carried the story across the nation, the group prepared to camp out on the island until the government acceded to their demand that it be converted into an Indian cultural center. Ninety years earlier, in 1879, a small band of Poncas broke away from their reservation in Indian Territory and, without official permission, headed north toward their ancestral home, traveling on foot in the winter cold and detouring around white settlements to avoid detection. Despite the gulf in time, the two events bear certain striking similarities. Both were conspicuous acts of defiance of the federal government; both represented assertions of basic Indian rights; both caught the imagination of the public and won widespread sympathy for the Indians in their fight for legal standing. But while the Alcatraz dispute was stalemated until the government forced evacuation of the island, the Ponca case ended in court and led to an unprecedented decision: for the first time Indians were established as persons under the terms of the Fourteenth Amendment.[1]

The opinion, which was handed down on May 12, 1879, by Judge Elmer Dundy of the United States District Court for Nebraska in the case popularly known as *Standing Bear* vs. *Crook*, was long overdue. Although non-tax-paying Indians had been excluded from citizenship by the first article of the Constitution, their exact legal status had never been clearly defined. The question may have been hypothetical in an earlier age when there was little contact between red man and white, but it took on increasing urgency after the mid-nineteenth century as a growing tide of white Americans moved out into the Indian country of the trans-Mississippi West.

At first the United States government simply avoided dealing on a personal basis with the original occupants of the continent. It negotiated with tribes as a whole, attempting to minimize friction between them and its own citizens by keeping the two groups apart. Under the terms of treaties like that signed with the Sioux and other plains tribes at Fort Laramie in 1851, it set aside large areas for the Indians and promised annuity payments in return for the right to build roads through them. Congress was often reluctant to ratify and fulfill the terms of such agreements, however, and impatient white settlers were inclined to respect them only when it was convenient to do so; in addition, the very concept of private property and of restricted hunting rights was alien to many Indian cultures.

1. Article 1 reads: "All persons born or naturalized in the United States, and subject to the jurisdiction thereof, are citizens of the United States and of the State wherein they reside. No State shall make or enforce any law which shall abridge the privileges or immunities of citizens of the United States; nor shall any State deprive any person of life, liberty, or property, without due process of law; nor deny to any person within its jurisdiction the equal protection of the laws."

As a result, the treaties were honored more in the breach than in the observance and wrong piled up on wrong and retaliation on retaliation.

By the end of the 1860s the "Indian question" had become a national issue. Westerners—particularly those who had been the victims of Indian depredations or who sought expansion into Indian lands—demanded immediate and massive military action to punish and subjugate the hostile tribes and remove them from the path of Manifest Destiny. Meanwhile, atrocities such as the 1864 massacre of peaceful Cheyennes and Arapahos at Sand Creek in Colorado Territory by a contingent of Colorado Volunteers prompted a congressional investigation, which attributed most Indian aggression to the lawlessness of whites. Furthermore, the existence of widespread graft in the transactions of the Indian Bureau promoted suspicions of an organized conspiracy, the nebulous "Indian Ring."

With the question of slavery settled, humanitarians—largely eastern clergymen and former abolitionists like Wendell Phillips—began to concern themselves with the Indian situation. Pointing to the government's bad faith in its relations with the tribes and what they saw as a vindictive policy of extermination, they called for major reform in the administration of Indian affairs. They believed—in the Social Darwinist sentiment of the time—that the Indians' only hope for survival was assimilation into the predominant society; and their program of civilization and christianization called for placing the Indians on reservations where they would be cared for by the government, sent to school, and taught the techniques of farming until they were ready to enter the mainstream of American life. Termination of the treaty system, the dissolution of tribal bonds, and the bestowal of full rights of citizenship on Indians were central to such a program.

In early 1869, even before his inauguration as president, Ulysses S. Grant acknowledged the need for reform in the Indian Service, and soon after he took office he announced a new approach to the administration of Indian affairs, the so-called Quaker and Peace policies. In an effort to eliminate corruption and to raise the moral level of bureau employees, the Quaker church would be allowed to nominate agents for certain tribes (other denominations later participated in the plan). The army, which had long thought it should have jurisdiction over the Indians, would act as a peacekeeping force, restricting the tribes to their reservations, by force if necessary, and preventing incursions on the reservations by whites. Designed to placate both sides in the controversy but never really satisfactory to either, these policies had essentially the same ultimate goal as the humanitarians: the mandatory transformation of the Indians into typical rural middle-class Americans.

The Poncas, a small, friendly tribe of village horticulturalists never numbering more than eight or nine hundred, seemed especially suited to such a program of acculturation. In 1858 they had accepted a reservation in the vicinity of their traditional homeland near the confluence of the Niobrara and Missouri rivers in present southeastern South Dakota. Despite occasional raids by their old enemies, the Sioux, they were reported to be making good progress in becoming civilized until 1868, when the reservation was inadvertently included in a large tract of land set aside for the Sioux. As the tempo of Sioux raids increased, the government apparently decided that it would be expedient to move them to Indian Territory, beyond the reach of their tormentors. Moreover, their relocation would fit in well with a scheme to concentrate all the tribes in one or two huge reserves where they would be easier to control and to protect from outsiders.

Although the Poncas opposed the plan—and could not legally, under the terms of the 1858 treaty, be moved without their permission—the move was carried out in 1877 under coercion. To compound the Indians' unhappiness, the trip was made under extraordinarily hard conditions and no preparations had been made for them in Indian Territory. A large number died during their first year there. In early 1879 one of the main chiefs, Standing Bear, and a band of followers left Indian Territory and returned homeward, stopping in Nebraska with the Omahas, who were closely allied to the Poncas.

Orders immediately went out to the commander of the Department of the Platte, Brigadier General George Crook at Fort Omaha, to take the runaway Poncas into custody and have them returned to their new reservation. A veteran of more than twenty years' service in the West, Crook had dealt with Indians from the Pacific Northwest to Arizona Territory and the northern plains. True, he was a noted Indian fighter, he had directed military campaigns against hostile tribes and felt that the War Department could work with the Indians more effectively than the Department of the Interior; yet he shared the humanitarians' views and aims. He had frequently come to the defense of his Indian wards when he felt they had been treated unfairly, and deplored the fraud and duplicity that so often characterized the government's relations with the tribes. Thus it was with great reluctance that he detailed a guard to arrest Standing Bear's party.

At this point the happenings at Fort Omaha came to the attention of the ebullient, volatile assistant editor of the *Omaha Daily Herald*, Thomas Henry Tibbles. An inveterate crusader, the thirty-nine-year-old Tibbles had served the abolitionist cause in Kansas Territory as a member of James Lane's Free-State Militia and after a Civil War career as a scout and newspaper correspondent had been a circuit-riding preacher in western Missouri and the Republican Valley of Nebraska. He had campaigned zealously in 1874 to raise relief funds for the victims of the grasshopper plague and had retired from the ministry three years later to become a full-time newspaperman. Now, on hearing the plight of the Poncas, he vowed to fight "for exactly the same principles for which he [had] fought twenty-four years ago, *the equality of all men before the law.*"

Securing the aid of two prominent Omaha lawyers, John L. Webster, a man in his early thirties who had practiced law in the city for some ten years, and Andrew J. Poppleton, a twenty-five-year resident who had served in the Nebraska territorial legislature and as mayor of Omaha, Tibbles arranged for a suit for a writ of habeas corpus to be brought in Standing Bear's name against General Crook. Crook was represented by the young district attorney for Nebraska, Genio M. Lambertson. The general cooperated completely in the proceedings; indeed, there is some evidence that he may have instigated them.[2] The plaintiff in the case was likely in his fifties at that time. Crook's aide-de-camp described him as a "noble looking *Indian*, tall and commanding in presence, dignified in manner."[3]

2. See the Note on the Text, p. 141.
3. Captain John G. Bourke, "Conference held between Brigadier General George Crook and a small band of Indians of the Ponca Tribe," insert following entry for September 9, 1878, Bourke Diary, United States Military Academy Library, West Point, New York.

The trial won wide notice as newspapers across the country followed its progress. It was unusual enough for an Indian to sue a general; but more than that, the case touched on one of the basic issues of the Indian problem: whether the civil liberties enjoyed by all other Americans were to be extended to the Indian. Tibbles wrote *The Ponca Chiefs* from his news stories in the *Omaha Daily Herald*. It was published pseudonymously in 1880, while he was lecturing in the East.[4] The book's impact is hard to estimate, but it seems reasonable to assume that the work was well known at least to the influential circle of reformers and to the audiences of Indian-rights sympathizers that Tibbles appeared before. For the modern reader it is of interest both as an eyewitness account of the famous trial and as a prime example of the humanitarian mentality. Standing Bear's story gives a familiar ring to the words of the youthful spokesman for the Alcatraz Indians: "We're talking about our right to live, our right to be people, and this is how [the government] respond[s]. . . . They've always dealt with us with a show of force. . . . We'll be back. America hasn't heard the last of its Indians."[5]

4. The Epilogue (p. 129) follows up the Ponca controversy and Tibbles's involvement in the Indian-rights movement after the trial. The Note on the Text (p. 138) discusses the origin and authoritativeness of the book as well as editorial alterations in this edition.

5. *New York Times*, June 20, 1971.

Dedication

THE PONCA CHIEFS

AN INDIAN'S ATTEMPT TO APPEAL FROM
THE TOMAHAWK TO THE COURTS

A FULL HISTORY OF THE ROBBERY OF THE PONCA
TRIBE OF INDIANS, WITH ALL THE PAPERS FILED
AND EVIDENCE TAKEN IN THE STANDING BEAR
HABEAS CORPUS CASE, AND FULL TEXT OF
JUDGE DUNDY'S CELEBRATED DECISION,
WITH SOME SUGGESTIONS TOWARDS A
SOLUTION OF THE INDIAN QUESTION

BY ZYLYFF

WITH AN INTRODUCTION BY
INSHTATHEAMBA (Bright Eyes)

AND DEDICATION BY
WENDELL PHILLIPS

Introduction

This little book is only a simple narration of facts concerning some of my people. Many of the transactions recorded in it came under my own observation, my uncle, White Swan, being one of the chiefs who underwent so much suffering after being left in the Indian Territory.

Wrongs more terrible than those related here have been practised on others of my people, but they have had no writer to make them known.

I wish for the sake of my race, that I could introduce this little book into every home in the land, because in these homes lies the power to remedy the evil shown forth in these pages. The people are the power which move the magistrates who administer the laws.

It is a little thing, a simple thing, which my people ask of a nation whose watchword is liberty; but it is endless in its consequences. They ask for their liberty, and law is liberty. "We did not know of these wrongs," say the magistrates. Is not that only the cry of "Am I my brother's keeper?" For years the petitions of my people have gone up unnoticed, unheeded by all but their Creator, and now at last a man of your race has arisen, who has shown faith enough in humanity to arouse the nation from the sin of its indifference. Thank God, it was only indifference, and not hatred, which withheld from an oppressed and unfortunate race, justice and mercy.

May those who read this story, when they think of the countless happy homes which cover this continent, give help to a homeless race, who have no spot on earth they can call their own.

INSHTATHEAMBA (Bright Eyes).

CHAPTER I

Standing Bear's First Encounter with the Indian Ring

In the autumn of 1876, the Indians on the Ponca reservation in Southern Dakota were at work on their farms as usual. It was as peaceful and happy a community as could be found anywhere. Most of their children were attending school, and their church was in a flourishing condition. How these people were robbed of their wealth and a large portion of them sent to their graves, through the tools of the Indian Ring, it is the object of these pages to relate.

One Sunday the Indians went to their church as usual, to hear the words of the minister, but some of the words which he said that tribe will never forget. He told them that he had heard that they were to be driven from their homes and sent far to the south, never to come back again. He said he was exceedingly sorry for them, as they had been honest, industrious, frugal, hard-working, and had just gotten themselves nice houses and farms. He did not know that he could help them. He could only pity them. Under all circumstances he advised them to do that which was right, and trust in God, that in the end he would protect them from their oppressors.

Consternation seized upon the whole community.

Runners were dispatched, and in a few hours afterwards every member of the Ponca tribe had heard the news. The one universal sentiment was: "We will not leave the home of our fathers to go to a strange land, never to return."

The chiefs and head men came together and questioned the minister, but he knew nothing more than he had already told. Somebody had ordered them to be taken to the Indian Territory.

Soon after a great council was called, and some men purporting to come from Washington appeared, and said an order had been issued to take the tribe to the Indian Territory. Standing Bear, White Eagle and other chiefs absolutely refused to go. Standing Bear said:

> This land is ours, we have never sold it. We have our houses and our homes here. Our fathers and some of our children are buried here. Here we wish to live and die. We have harmed no man. We have kept our treaty. We have learned to work. We can make a good living here. We do not wish to sell our land, and we think no man has a right to take it from us. Here we will live, and here we will die.

Then these men told them that the Indian Territory was a much better country. That they could raise much more grain and not work near so hard. That if they once saw it they would not want to stay in Dakota, and many other things of like nature. Finally, they proposed that the chiefs should go down to the Indian Territory and look at the country. Then, if they did not like it, and did not wish to go, they might stay where they were. They told them that if they went down there, the Great Father would buy their land in Dakota and pay them for it, and give them all the land they needed in the Indian Territory.

If they would just go down and look at the country all
the trouble would be ended. They could sell their land
then or not, just as they pleased. After further consultation
it was agreed that ten of the leading men should go down
there and look at the country.

These men took them to the territory. They showed
them a portion of country, and wanted to know what
they thought of it. The chiefs replied they did not like it
at all. They did not think it was as good as where they
were located in Dakota. Standing Bear's account of what
occurred at this time is as follows:

These men then talked entirely different from what they did
in Dakota. They said, you *shall* trade your land in Dakota for
land here. You can go out there and choose what you want, but
you *shall trade.* Your tribe will be brought down here, and you
may as well choose your land now. I told them that we could
not come. I had seen that a great many people down there were
sick. The land they showed us was stony, and I did not believe
we could make a living on it. I was afraid my people would
get sick and die. We could not come there.

Then the men grew very angry, and said if we did not agree
to come they would go off and leave us there to starve. They
would not take us back home. We said it would be better for
ten of us to die than that the whole tribe, all the women and little
children, should be brought there to die, and die we all would,
right there, rather than do what they asked.

Then they went off and said we might stay there and die.
They would not take us back. I sent the interpreter to them,
and told them that they had brought us far from our own
country on the cars, and if they would not take us back they
should at least give us some money to pay our way. They said
they would not give me one cent of money. They had said they
would take us from the Indian Territory to see the Great Father.
I sent and asked if they would take us to Washington, and told

them if they would, and the Great Father said we must come to
the Indian Territory, then, I supposed, we must come. They
replied that the Great Father had nothing to do with the matter.
They would not take us anywhere. We could stay there and die.
I sent again, and told them if they would not take us back, nor
give us any money, to give us a paper that we could show to
white men and tell who we were, so they would not think we
were hostile or intended to steal from them. They replied they
would give us nothing, not even a paper.

Now, there were two very old men with us, who could not
travel on foot at all. I sent to them and told them we would walk
back, but that these two old men could not walk and they must
care for them. We could not carry them on our backs, and they
must take them, and I sent the old men to them, and told them to
stay with them. They took these two old men and went off and
left us.

None of us had a cent of money, and we had no interpreter,
so we could not speak a word to any man. The next morning we
started on our long journey. It was in the winter. White men
were suspicious of us. They thought we were vagabond Indians,
who will travel round to beg and won't work. Very few of them
would give us anything. Every day we travelled on we grew
weaker, and had to go slower. We got a few pieces of bread.
What we lived on was corn. We would take it and pound it
between stones. We slept out on the prairie without shelter.
A few times we found haystacks to sleep in. It took us just fifty
days to reach the Otoe Agency in Southern Nebraska. The last
few days we were very weak, and could walk only a few miles.
When we got there, we found that these men had sent word to
the Agent there to have nothing to do with us; that we were bad
Indians, and if we came there we should be driven off. But when
the Agent saw how nearly starved we were, and looked at our
bleeding feet, for our moccasins wore out the first ten days, he
took pity on us, and first gave us something to eat, and then
asked us what bad things we had been doing. When we told him
what had happened, he was much astonished, and said he would

write a letter to Washington, and tell all how we had been treated.

The Otoes gave us horses and provisions, and we made the journey to the Omaha Agency in five days. We looked so bad when we got there that everybody was sorry for us. From there we sent a telegram to the President. The other seven who were with me went on up to the reservation on horseback, and Mr. Hamilton, the missionary to the Omahas, sent John Springer, an educated Omaha, with me to Sioux City to send the telegram. We stopped at the first station at which we reached the railroad, and sent the telegram. It cost $6.25. We asked the operator who sent it if anybody would stop it before it got to Washington, and he said, "No, if they did, they would be put out of their place."

John Springer went on with me to Sioux City, and we went to see the editor of the paper there *(Sioux City Journal)*. We told him all about it, and he printed it in his paper. Springer gave me some money there, and left me, and I went on the cars up to Yankton. The men who took us to the Territory had returned and were there. A white man, whom I did not know, came to me there, and said he had heard about our troubles. He said these men who were there were scoundrels. He knew every one of them. They were very bad men who got rich by swindling the Indians. He said he knew that we had never sold our land, or signed a treaty to go away, and the best thing for me was to go back to my farm, go to work, and pay no attention to what these men said, or what orders they gave, until some man came who had papers signed by the President. He said if these men had land, and another man should come and order them to leave it, they would knock him down, and that was the way they ought to be served!

I went back to the Ponca Agency and these same men came there. They wanted to talk again. I said: "What are you here for? What business have you to come here at all. I never sent for you. I don't want anything to do with you. You are all liars. You are all bad men. You have no authority from the Great

Father. You came out here to cheat and steal. You can read and write, and I can't, and you think you know everything and I know nothing. If some man should take you a thousand miles from home, as you did me, and leave you in a strange country without one cent of money, where you did not know the language and could not speak a word, you would never have got home in the world. You don't know enough. I want you to go off of this reservation. You have no business here, and don't come back until you bring a letter from the Great Father. Then if you want to buy my land, bring the money with you so I can see it. If I want to sell I will talk to you. If I don't I won't. This is my land. The Great Father did not give it to me. My people were here and owned this land before there was any Great Father. We sold him some land, but we never sold this. This is mine. God gave it to me. When I want to sell it I will let you know. You are a rascal and a liar, and I want you to go off my land. If you were treating a white man the way you are treating me, he would kill you, and everybody would say he did right. I will not do that. I will harm no white man, but this is my land, and I intend to stay here and make a good living for my wife and children. You can go."

When I said this he was very angry, and the next morning he had Big Snake and me arrested. They took us down to Yankton, and brought us before eight officers. The head officer said: "We have heard many complaints about you. We have had four letters making complaints. What have you to say? I thought you were good and all trying to work. I have read in the papers that you have been badly treated, but these letters say exactly the opposite."

Then we told the soldiers all about it, and the soldiers were angry at what had been done, and the head officer said: "I will send a telegram to Washington, but you will stay here until I hear from it. I will not put you in prison. That land is yours. I have a hard duty, but I am a soldier, and must obey orders. I would like to help you, but I cannot. I have known your tribe a long time, and you have all done well, and learned how to work. I know that is so. Some rascals are trying to swindle you out of your land and stock. I have seen things like this many times. It is very hard to see this, but I can't help it. When a white man has land he can stay on it, and if anybody else wants it they have to pay him money for it, and he don't have to give it up until he gets the money, and I don't see why the same law will not apply to an Indian who has land."

The soldiers treated us very kindly, and after a little while we went back on the reservation. I don't know whether the head officer ever had from Washington an answer from his telegram. Then these men got up another council. The half-breeds who belong to the tribe are most all bad men; they are rascals, and go with the agents and traders. At this council all the half-breeds took the side of these men. They all wanted to go to the Indian Territory. But not one of the Poncas would agree to go. At this council there was a white man who came to talk for us. He was a lawyer, and said he had been watching us for years, and he knew we were trying to do right. He said he would not see us swindled out of all we had, and not do anything.

These men said to us that we were thieves and bad Indians, and the Commissioner had resolved to move us away from the white people. That the Sioux would come and kill us all unless they kept many soldiers to watch them, and that cost the Great Father much money, and that he did not have many soldiers any more, and what he had he wanted to fight for the white people, and not to protect bad Indians.

Then this lawyer answered back for us. He said he did not want to call them liars, but he believed they were. If they had any authority for what they were doing, why did they not show the papers. They had none. They could not show an order of any kind. He would not say so positively, but he believed they were all of the same lot of thieves who had always been swindling the Indians. That reservation belonged to the Poncas. They had never gone to war with the whites, though everybody knew they had cause enough. Nobody could take it from them. Nobody could make them sell it. Even the Great Father could not do that. He said many other things, and talked a long while. He got very angry at last, and said they were thieves and scoundrels, and if they were served right they would every one be hung. Then they would not let him talk any more.

At last they said it was no use to talk any more. We must all go to the Indian Territory, and that was the end of the matter. It was no use for us to say we would not, because we *must*. We told them we would not go, and the council broke up.

Soon after this the half-breeds belonging to the tribe, numbering ten men and their families, packed up and started. This white lawyer told us not to go, and he did not believe they would try to make us go. He said for us to do what we thought best, and not rely on him, but it was his belief that if we went on with our work and paid no attention to them they would not do anything. He said, "If you want to go, go, and if you don't, stay right where you are. It will be time enough when they begin to try to make you go. Nobody will shoot you while you are at work. If the soldiers come and give you orders, then you will have to obey."

We talked over the matter very much, and we were very sad. After a little while some soldiers came to the Agency, and the interpreter said they had come to go to war with us, if we did not go. We could not fight. We were all farming and had but few guns. Everybody was working hard. It was in the spring. Many had sowed their spring wheat, some had planted corn, and made gardens. The children were going to school. One day about noon, I had just come in from the field; my brother was still at work, and another man was plowing for me. My wife was getting dinner, and a man rode up. He said the officer had given an order that we were to load up everything we had and bring it to the Agency building. I supposed it came from the soldiers, and I unhitched my horses from the plows and hitched them to the wagons, and loaded in all I had. There were some things the government had given us. I do not count them. They had given them to us, and I suppose they had the right to take them back.

Among them were the threshing machines, reapers, mowers, and the mill. Then I had some things which I had bought with the grain and stock I had raised and sold. These were mine, and no man had any right to take them away. However, I obeyed the order, and took them all to the Agency. Within two or three days I had them all there. These were the things which were mine and which they took away:

One house (I built it with my own hands. It took me a long time, for I didn't know how very well). It was twenty feet by forty, with two rooms; four cows, three steers, eight horses, four hogs (two very large ones), five wagon-loads of corn with the side boards on (about 130 bushels), one hundred sacks of wheat, and one wagon-load loose, which I had in boxes (about 275 bushels), twenty-one chickens, two turkeys, and one prairie breaking plow, two stirring plows, two corn plows, a good stable and cattle sheds, three axes, two hatchets, one saw, three lamps, four chairs, one table, two new bedsteads, one hay-knife, three pitchforks, two washtubs, and washboard, one cross-cut saw, one cant hook, two log chains, two ox-yokes, two ladders, two garden rakes, three hoes, one new cooking-stove, one heating-stove, twenty joints of pipe, two trunks (one very large), one valise, crockery, knives and forks, and a great many other things which I cannot now remember. These things were mine. I had worked for them all. By their order I brought them all, except the house and such things as I could not move, to the Agency, and they put them in a big house and locked them up. I have never seen any of them since. Our wagons and ponies they did not take away.

A few days after this we started to the Indian Territory. I said I would not go there when I started. If some man wanted my things and my land, I said I would go down and live among the Omahas. They wanted us all to come there, and had land enough for all. The man who had charge of us said we could go down there where the other part of the tribe was and see them, and if we did not like it, we could then come back to the Omahas.

My wife had some relations who went down with the half-breeds, and she wanted to go and see them, and so we went on. It was a long and tedious journey. When we got there the Agent issued us no rations for a long time. For months we had to beg of the other tribes. We were all half-starved. This was all different from our own home. There we raised all we needed. Here there was no work to do. We had nothing to work with, and there was no man to hire us. We said we would go back; that we did not like it there. Then we were informed that we were prisoners, and if we attempted to go away from the Agency we would be punished. Sickness commenced, several died. All my people were heart-broken. I was like a child. I could not help even myself, much less help them. I hunted for some white man, who knew the ways of the government, to tell me what to do. No man would tell me. At last I resolved I would go and see the Great Father. I thought surely he does not know about this. He would never allow it to be done. I went to see the Great Father and told him what had been done. He seemed very much astonished. He said he never heard of it before. He would order it investigated. Then I talked with him again. He thought now that we were down there we had better stay. He told me to go back and hunt for some good land, and he would have our things sent to us; that we should be treated well, and he did not think we would be sick any more, after a little. We would soon get used to the country, and then we would not be sick. I said in reply that I could only obey his orders.

Then I went back to the Indian Territory and selected some land that looked good, and we moved the tribe on to it. It was now in the fall, and the sickness was worse than ever. Families had settled on separate tracts of land, and were scattered around. The whole family would be sick and no one know it. In some of these families persons would die and the others would not be able to bury them. They would drag them with a pony out on the prairie and leave them there. Men would take sick while at work and die in less than a day (congestive chills).

There were dead in every family. Those who could walk around were sick. Not one in the whole tribe felt well. I lost all my children but one little girl. A few more weeks and she would have died too. I was in an awful place, and I was a prisoner there. I was not a free man. I had been taken by force from my own country to a strange land, and was a captive. Sometimes I thought I had better gather up my people, send them on ahead, keep my warriors in the rear, and endeavor to retreat to the mountains, and if the soldiers came, all die fighting, but I did not want to fight the soldiers. They had always treated me kindly, and the officers had taken my part; besides my warriors were too sick to march or fight. I could see nothing ahead, but death for the whole tribe. I was much sorry for the little children who were so very sick. They would moan and moan, and we had no medicine and no way to help them. The fall months wore away, and it was the middle of winter. The sickness got no better. I resolved at last that I would make an attempt to save the lives of a few. If I failed it could be no worse than to stay there. I said I will take a small party and start back to my old home. If the soldiers come after us I will not fight. They can do what they please with us. Whatever they do, it can't be worse than to stay here. I told nobody of my plans but those I intended to take along. I brought away thirty persons, seven of whom were very sick when we started. We slipped away on the night of the second of January. We had a small quantity of rations when we started. I had ten dollars in money, and Buffalo Chip had ten. We were ten weeks making the journey to the Omaha Agency. I had to buy a little corn for the ponies.

We had three covered wagons and one light spring wagon. I subsisted this party of thirty persons for twenty days on less than a dollar a day. After that we had no more money. For two days we were without food, little children, sick, and all. Then I went to a white man's house and motioned for him to come with me. He came and I pointed out to him the sick. He did not seem to understand, but he looked at the ponies and saw how very poor and gaunt they were. He went off and came back with his boys and brought hay and a big bag full of corn. We took some of the corn, shelled and parched it. He watched us, and when he saw the children eat it ravenously, he, for the first time, seemed to understand that we had nothing to eat. He went to the house and brought us some flour, some meat and some coffee. After that the white people treated us very kindly. Some gave us bread, some coffee, and others meal or flour. None of them refused to give us anything when they saw we were hungry, except two places, and I don't think they had much themselves. I kept far out in Kansas, and frequently changed my course, for I thought they would follow us from the Agency, and the white people out there seemed very poor. After ten weeks of such journeying, about the middle of March we arrived at the Omaha Agency, on the way back to our old home. The Omahas and Poncas speak the same language, and we have many relatives among them. We intended to go back to our own land, but the Omahas said, you have no plows or tools of any kind, and you cannot go back there. We will lend you seed and tools to work with, and help you start. They gave us land. There was enough broken to raise what we wanted to live on. Some of the men were sick in bed and couldn't work. Those who were well enough all went to work. Some had sowed their spring wheat, and some were plowing. I was at work when the runner came and told us that the soldiers had come to take us back. Consternation and despair seized upon us. We all went down to the Agency, and found Lieut. Carpenter there. He said we must go to Omaha with him, and there we could talk with Gen. Crook. We hitched up our ponies and started south again. One woman was too sick to move, and that one was left at the Agency, and came to Omaha barracks. When we started back the scene among the women and children was heart-rending. They and their friends among the Omahas cried most bitterly. It would break one's heart to look at them. Many were still sick, and all felt that we were going back to certain death. My efforts to save their lives had failed.

INTERPRETER'S CERTIFICATE

I certify that I acted as interpreter for Standing Bear, and that the above is a true translation of his words, the interview taking place at Fort Omaha the 13th day of April, 1879. I am perfectly acquainted with the Omaha Indian language, which the Poncas speak, and I know many of the facts to be true of my own knowledge, having resided among the Omahas for twelve years.

W. W. HAMILTON

CHAPTER II

Standing Bear Finds a Friend in the Editor of a Western Paper

On the twenty-ninth day of March, 1879, at about eleven o'clock at night, there sat in the editorial room of the *Omaha Daily Herald* the assistant editor, who at the time was editor-in-chief.

The city editor came in and informed him that he had just returned from Fort Omaha, four miles distant, where there was a band of Ponca Indians under arrest for running away from the Indian Territory.

This assistant editor of the *Herald* had a strange history. He said he had been born on the frontier, never had had any raising, and did not pretend to be civilized. He was a thorough newspaper man, and had held positions as an editorial writer on several leading papers. He had the medical, legal, theological, turf, stage and musical terms at his tongue's end. He carried perhaps the marks of more gunshot and other wounds on his person than any other one man in a thousand miles of him. He was one of the best shots with a revolver in the west. He commenced life by enlisting in Jim Lane's company in Kansas in 1856, and was in every prominent fight during the bloody wars which lasted for two years in that Territory. Part of the time he was in old John Brown's company. Such was the individual who sat at the *Herald* editoral table on that night. When informed of what had occurred at the barracks, he brought his fist down on the table and said, "Those Indians shall not be taken back to die in the Indian Territory."

He was doing nearly double work on the paper on account of the absence of the editor-in-chief, and his duties kept him at the office until the paper went to press at four o'clock in the morning. That morning he retired at 4:30 A.M., and rose at seven A.M., and immediately started on foot to Fort Omaha, four miles distant. It was on Sunday, and while others went to church he went to see these prisoners. Arriving there he found an interpreter, and informed Standing Bear that he wanted to hold a council and print what he said, so that all the white people could know how he had been treated. But Standing Bear would not talk. He did not think it would be dignified for him to talk with any one else before he held his council with Gen. Crook. Persuasion did no good. He was afraid Gen. Crook would take it as an insult, and talk he would not. It was explained to him that it would not be printed until Tuesday morning, that no paper was published on Monday, but it was all of no avail.

Here was something that the editor had not expected, an impassable barrier on the first day's march, and he sat down and cogitated. At last he remembered that several years before he had joined a secret society among the Indians, and concluded to try the signs on the old chief. Standing Bear recognized them in an instant, and the two gave the grip of friendship. A council was called immediately, and the editor and warriors were soon seated in a tepee around the council fire smoking the pipe of peace.

Ta-zha-but (Buffalo Chip) was the first to speak. He

talked slowly, making graceful but emphatic gestures, as follows:

TA-ZHA-BUT'S SPEECH

I sometimes think that the white people forget that we are human, that we love our wives and children, that we require food and clothing, that we must take care of our sick, our women and children, prepare not only for the winters as they come, but for old age when we can no longer do as when we are young. But one Father made us all. We have hands and feet, heads and hearts all alike. We also are men. Look at me. Am I not a man? I am poor. These clothes are ragged. I have no others. But I am a man.

Ta-zha-but stopped after saying this, for several moments, and all was as silent as death. He then proceeded:

I have said this, because as I have been sitting in this tepee thinking since I was taken prisoner, that the government could not think I was a man, or they would not treat me as they have. I have hands that know how to hold the plow handles and to sow the wheat and corn and gather it in. I have taught them that in the last few years.

When I was young the gun was the greatest friend the Indian had. With it he defended himself against his enemies, with it he fed his wife and family, covered his tepee, and clothed himself and his children. The gun is not my friend now. The greatest friend I have is the plow. The game is gone, never to come back. I look everywhere and I see none. It has vanished away like a dream when I wake from sleep. But the ground is here. It can never vanish away. From the ground the Indian must live. It tells him no lies. It makes him no promises which it does not fulfil. It is like Wakanda. All the Indians know this. They are not blind, that they cannot see. Neither are they fools, that they cannot think. So we talked among ourselves years ago. We agreed that we would raise cattle, horses, pigs, and all kinds of stock. We said we would learn to plow, we would build houses out of wood, we would learn to do like the white people. They always have good clothes and enough to eat. We told the men the Great Father sent to talk to us that we would do this years ago. We have kept our word. We have taught our hands to hold the plow handles. We built houses. We raised stock. Now look at us to-day. See these rags. We have no houses, no stock, no grain, we are prisoners in this camp, and we have never committed any crime.

Here another prolonged silence ensued, and then Ta-zha-but spoke again:

Eight days ago I was at work on my farm which the Omahas gave me. I had sowed some spring wheat, and wished to sow some more. I was living peaceably with all men. I have never committed any crime. I was arrested and brought back as a prisoner. Does your law do that? I have been told since the great war that all men were free men, and that no man can be made a prisoner unless he does wrong. I have done no wrong, and yet I am here a prisoner. Have you a law for white men, and a different law for those who are not white?

Ta-zha-but paused and waited for a reply. The editor found himself cornered. The Declaration of Independence says "all men are created equal." The constitution says there shall be no distinction on account of race or color, but here was a man who had committed no crime, held as a prisoner. He at last replied that there was but one law for all alike.

Ta-zha-but. —"Then why am I and my family held prisoners when we have committed no crime?"

Editor. —"I cannot tell."

Another silence here fell on the council. The Indians sat smoking a huge tomahawk pipe, and passing it one to another. Ta-zha-but spoke again:

When I worked my farm, my wife, my children and myself
had three meals each day. When I am forced to live on the government we get but one. Why does the government insist on
feeding me? If they intend to always feed all the Indians I should
think they would eat all the government had. I seem to be blind.
I cannot understand these things. Here I am, and those who are
with me want to go to work and raise grain to live on next winter. We don't want to live on the government. We want to support ourselves. We commence to plow and sow wheat, and the
government sends the soldiers to take us prisoners and make us
live on the government. We would go right back to our work
and make our own living if they would only let us.

This declaration of the chief was received by an emphatic affirmative grunt by all present. Ta-zha-but then
asked if it would not be better for the government and
them, to be allowed to pursue such a course, and why they
could not do it. The editor could give no reason why
they should not.

"If we go back to the reservation in the Indian Territory," said Ta-zha-but, "we shall have nothing to do.
We must live on the government and will soon all die.
There will be not one left to tell the tale. It would be better
for the government, better for us, to stand us out there in
a line, bring the soldiers and tell them to shoot us all.
Then our miseries would be ended, and the government
would have no more trouble. It would be better that way."

This was said in a solemn tone, spoken very slowly,
and every one present signified his assent. Somehow a
feeling of solemnity came over all. They seemed to think
death was very near in any event. A squaw who held a
young baby, sitting behind the men, pressed the little
thing close to her bosom and rocked herself back and
forth, with the tears running down over her face. Not a

muscle moved on the face of any of the men. They looked steadily toward the fire in the centre of the lodge. The first thing that was said was by Charles Morgan, an Omaha, who reads and writes, and speaks English as fluently as any one. He turned to the reporter, after some moments of silence, and said: "This is awful. These men are my friends. They are of my blood."

The editor after a few moments asked Ta-zha-but what he thought ought to be done in reference to the Indians, how the government should deal with them. He continued as follows:

It seems to me that the government should let the Indians go on some land that is good, where good crops could be raised. This land should be given them for theirs forever, given so that the government could not take it away, so that the white men could not get it. It should be the Indians' forever. Indians cannot make plows and axes and wagons, so the government should give them some to help them start. All the Indians will go to farming if the government will do this. But they can't farm without plows, and they can't plow where the ground is all hills and stones like it is down where the Ponca reservation was. Then there should be laws to govern the Indians the same as the whites. A court should be established where those who do wrong, both Indians and white men, should be tried. There never would be any rows or troubles with the whites if we had a court. But we have never had a court. If white men steal our ponies there is nobody to punish them. If the Indians do wrong they make the tribe responsible and the soldiers come out and kill our people. We want land which shall be our own, and we want a court. Let those who do right be protected, and those who do wrong be punished. If the Indian has land which he knows is his own forever, he will build a good house. He will soon be like a white man.

STANDING BEAR'S SPEECH

Standing Bear spoke as follows:

The Poncas and the Omahas are one tribe, and speak exactly
the same language. We saw the game was gone some years
ago, and we resolved to go to farming, to raise stock and grain
like the white men. Our Agency was in the edge of Dakota.
We had many good farms, some good houses, a school and a
church. But the Sioux made raids on us, stole some of our ponies,
and killed some of our people. It was then proposed that we
come down to the Omaha agency. There was a great council
of the Poncas, the Omahas, and the Commissioners the Great
Father sent. Both the Omahas and Poncas signed a paper to
go to the Omaha Agency. *That is all the paper we ever signed.*

Then followed a history, stated briefly, of what had
occurred as narrated at length in the first chapter. He
proceeded as follows:

We were taken to the Indian Territory. My son died, my
sister died, and my brother there, was near dying. We had
nothing to do but sit still, be sick, starve and die. I know I never
signed a paper to go there, and after many months of a life that
was more than to die, we concluded to come to our relations
and friends the Omahas. We brought our sick with us. The
weather was very bad and we have little clothes. We had very
little to eat on the way and were very hungry, but we never
touched anything that belonged to a white man. I am getting
old now, he is old (pointing to his brother). We have but a little
time to live. My son who died was a good boy. I did everything
I could to help educate him, that when I was gone he could live
like the white men and teach these little ones (pointing to some
little children). I am too old to learn to read and write and count
money. They can learn. I want to work on a farm, have them
go to school, learn many things, and be like white children. I

know how to plow, how to plant wheat and corn, to raise stock. The Omahas gave me some land with thirty acres broke. I can raise this year enough wheat, potatoes and other things to have plenty to eat next winter. But the government won't let me. My boy who died down there, as he was dying looked up to me and said, I would like you to take my bones back and bury them there where I was born. I promised him I would. I could not refuse the dying request of my boy. I have attempted to keep my word. His bones are in that trunk.

At this point Standing Bear's wife, who is a very intelligent-looking woman, asked permission to speak to the editor. Her eyes were full of tears. She said:

My mother is buried there, my grandmother and another child. My boy was a good boy, and we tried to do what he wanted us to do. We were just getting ready to bury him, when the soldiers came upon us. Won't you go to Gen. Crook and ask him, if we must go back south, to let us have time to take him back to the Agency and bury him?

A promise was made to the weeping mother that such a request would be made. She said:

My heart is broken. My eyes are full of tears all the time, and ever since I came to this place there is an ache here (laying her hand on her heart). If we must go back these little children will soon die too.

A long silence followed. The mother sat there with features immovable, but the tears chased one another in quick succession down her cheeks. Such a feeling of depression and utter hopelessness settled down over all that the editor arose and left the lodge and walked around outside a few minutes. When he went back, Standing Bear continued:

When Big-White-Hair (Senator Saunders) and the other commissioners came down there last summer, he asked if we desired to be turned over to the military.* I told him I did not like to say certainly. I could not read nor talk English, and there were so many Indians of different tribes, and so many goods to be brought to the reservations that there must be many things I did not know anything about. The Indians all thought that if they were turned over to the soldiers they would get all the government gave to them, while with the agents and traders they did not. But some of the Indians were afraid if the soldiers had control and any of the young men did anything wrong they would be too severe. All the Indians who have reservations of good land would now raise enough to support themselves if it were not for the agents and traders. They don't want the Indians to become like white men. They are the worst thing in the way of the Indians. All the Indians know the game is gone. They want land of their own, they want schools, they want to learn to work. Wakanda knows I tell the truth. (This sentence was said with an upward look and reverent gesture.) We want to be under the same law as the white man. We want to be free. The northern tribes who have been sent south will all die. All they ask is that they may have a chance to make a living for themselves, and have the same law as the white man.

It was explained to him that if he came under the law he would have to pay taxes. He thought it over a minute or two, and then said:

I don't think for the first year or two we ought to pay taxes. We would have very little to pay with, but after that, if

*[In 1878 Senator Alvin Saunders of Nebraska served on a joint congressional committee studying the question of transferring the Bureau of Indian Affairs from the Department of the Interior to the War Department. The bureau had been in the War Department until the establishment of the Department of the Interior in 1849, and proposals to transfer it back were offered periodically for several decades thereafter.—*ed. note*]

the officers would protect us from bad white men, and punish those who steal, so all our property would be safe, then we could afford to pay for it, and let every man pay according to how much he had. If the Indians are given lands and courts, with the same law as the white man, a few plows to start with, and a school teacher for the children, they need not be turned over to the soldiers, the civil authorities, or anybody else. That will be the end of all our troubles. Ten years from now there will be no difference from the whites except in the color of their skin.

After Standing Bear had closed his speech, the editor came outside of the lodge. The sun was just sinking in the west. The city laid four miles away. There was no way to get there but to walk there. Not a mouthful of food had he taken since morning, but he thrust his note-book in his pocket and struck out on a five-miles-an-hour gait for the city. He had an idea in his head, and there was no time to lose. He resolved he would lay the matter before as many of the churches as he could reach that night, and get them to pass a resolution requesting the Secretary of the Interior to rescind the order, and then send a telegram to Washington. To do it, he must reach the city before the hour set for services to commence. By the end of the first mile it began to grow dark, and he found he must make faster time than that. Not a single vehicle was going in that direction, although he met several going the other way. He leaned forward and broke into a regular Rowell run, which he did not break until he had made two miles and a half. He reached the Presbyterian church, Rev. Mr. Harsha pastor, just in time, and obtained permission to speak after the sermon. He then went to the Congregational Church, Rev. Mr. Sherrill pastor, and spoke between the opening hymns. Both of the churches passed a resolution requesting Mr. Carl

Schurz to rescind the order under which this band of
Poncas were being returned to Indian Territory.

Other ministers were afterward seen, and Rev. Mr.
Jameson, who was an old friend and acquaintance of Mr.
Schurz, wrote the following, which was signed and sent
by telegraph:

OMAHA, NEB., March, 31, 1879.
To Hon. Carl Schurz, Secretary of the Interior, Washington,
*   D.C.:*

Seven lodges of Ponca Indians, who had settled on Omaha
reservation, and were commencing to work at farming, have,
by your order, been arrested to be taken south. I beseech you
as a friend to have this order revoked. Several churches and
congregations have passed resolutions recommending that these
Indians be permitted to remain with the Omahas. Some of the
Indians are too sick to travel. Particulars by mail.

E. H. E. JAMESON,
Pastor Baptist Church.

We concur in the above.

H. D. FISHER,
Pastor M. E. Church.
W. J. HARSHA,
Pastor Presbyterian Church.
A. F. SHERRILL,
Pastor Congregational Church.

At eleven o'clock that night the weary editor reached
his home. The first thing he did was to call for a good
"square meal." Having disposed of that he sat down at
his desk and wrote out the speeches of Standing Bear and
Ta-zha-but, with such other matter as made a connected
history of the affair up to that time and at twenty minutes
past 5 A.M. retired.

At seven o'clock he was up. Gen. Crook was to hold

his council with Standing Bear at ten o'clock, and pro-
curing a conveyance, he started for Fort Omaha.   The
council did not really commence until twelve o'clock,
and was held in Gen. Crook's office.   There were present
General Crook, Colonel Royall, General Williams, Lieu-
tenants Bourke and Carpenter, and the editor, who was
somewhat astonished to see Standing Bear dressed in a
magnificent full costume of an Indian chief.   He had a
red blanket, trimmed with broad blue stripes, a wide
beaded belt around his waist, and wore a necklace of bear's
claws.   The other Indians were dressed in citizens' clothes.
Standing Bear spoke first as follows:

FRIENDS AND BROTHERS, — The Almighty created us Indians.
We are as he made us. The Almighty has given to the whites a
book to read, and they have plenty of things to work with.
The Indian has no book. He cannot read. Here is where I am
weak and you are strong. I never see a book or paper of any
kind, but I think it is a good thing. It lets you know all that
is going on in the world. I want my children to learn to read.
I want them to go to school, my friends. A great while ago we
came from the great water to the east. We kept coming, coming,
coming west until we got to Dakota. I made a good living there.
Then some power took hold of me, as by the arm, and made
me to stand up and told us to go south. They took us to a very
bad place. They took our plows and all our farming utensils
and locked them up. I have never seen them since. After I got
to the Territory I went to see my Great Father at Washington.
When I went into his office he took me by the hand. I said to
the Great Father, "My people are much wronged, and I hope
you will do something for me. I am in an awful bad place."
I told him before I went to the Territory that I had a good house
and barn which I had built with my own hands. I had cattle
and hogs and all kinds of stock, and somebody came and took
all my things away, and my Great Father stood up and said:

"How is this? I will order an inspection." I told him I was in a bad fix. He told me to go and see if I could find some good land near where we then were. I went back. I started to look for land. I found some land that looked good. We moved onto it, but some unseen force came down upon us and crushed us to the earth. One hundred and fifty-seven of our people died right there. A few days passed by, and an inspector came from Washington. I told him I would like to move back to my old home, that he saw we were in a dreadful place. He answered in this way: "I will do all I can. I will try what I can do for you." He didn't say he could do anything, but that he would go back to Washington, and tell them what a bad place it was. But I was like one in haste. I wanted to save the lives of my people.

Standing Bear then asked permission to address the officers and others present, and Gen. Crook gave him permission, and turning to them, he made the following pathetic appeal:

MY FRIENDS AND BROTHERS, —I am now with the soldiers and officers. I want to go back to my old place north. I want to save myself and my tribe.

My brothers, it seems to me as if I stood in front of a great prairie fire. I would take up my babies and run to save their lives; or as if I stood on the bank of an overflowing river, and I would take my people and fly to higher ground. Oh! my brothers, the Almighty looks down on me, and knows what I am, and hears my words. May the Almighty send a good spirit to brood over you, my brothers, to move you to help me. If a white man had land, and some one should swindle him, that man would try to get it back, and you would not blame him. Look on me. Take pity on me, and help me to save the lives of the women and children. My brothers, a power, which I cannot resist, crowds me down to the ground. I need help. I have done.

TA-ZHA-BUT'S SPEECH
In the start I knew nothing of what was going on. I was hold-

ing the handles of my plow. I had a home. I built a good stable. I raised cattle and hogs and all kinds of stock. I broke land. All these things I lost by some bad man. Any one knows to take a man from a cold climate, and put him in the hot sun down in the south it would kill him. We refused to go down there. We afterwards went down to see our friends, and see how they liked it. Brothers, I come home now. I took my brothers and friends and came back here. We went to work. I had hold of the handles of my plow. It looks this way: The government wants me to go back, but I think it would be a better plan for me to go to work and raise something to live on next winter. Down there it weakens me all over. My hands drop down by my sides, and I cannot use them. We all feel sick all the time. I desire to stay here, where I can work and raise plenty to eat for my family.

Gen. Crook.—"How long since you went down there?"
Answer.—"In 1877, May or June."
Gen. Crook.—"I have heard all this story before. It is just as they represent it. It has long since all been reported to Washington."
Gen. Crook, turning to Standing Bear, said:

It is a very hard case, but I can do nothing myself. I have received an order from Washington and I must obey it. They have all the facts in Washington, and it would do no good for me to intercede. I might send a telegram, but it is likely to do more harm than good. They can stay here a few days and let their stock strengthen up.

Standing Bear then said he would like to say a few more words, and General Crook gave him permission. He said:

I have been going around for three years. I have lost all my property. My constant thought is, "What man has done this?" Of course I know I cannot say "no." Whatever they say I must do, I must do it. I know you have an order to send me to the

Indian Territory, and we must obey it. I have this request to make. The Great Father orders us to go back to the Indian Territory. He should give us some money to pay our expenses and buy such things as we need on the way. Half of my people here are sick, and of course they will die before we get there, and they must be buried. I wish the Great Father would give us money to pay the necessary expenses.

Gen. Crook.—"All we can do is to give you what rations you will require on the way down. You will be permitted to take all your stock with you, and you can go slowly. It is a very disagreeable duty to send you down there, but I must obey orders."

At the close of the council Lieut. Carpenter reported to General Crook that six of the Indians were very sick and needed medical attention. Gen. Crook made some inquiries and found the post surgeon had prescribed for them that morning.

It was nearly three o'clock when the editor reached his office. He first wrote out the speeches and Gen. Crook's reply, and then made arrangements to have them telegraphed to different papers in New York, Chicago and other cities. Then he sat himself down and wrote three columns of editorial matter for the paper in the morning. At 3:30 A.M. he stretched himself out on his bed for a sleep, remarking that he had made some hard campaigns for the liberty of black men with pistol and sabre, but this campaign for the liberty of the Indian, in which the pen was the only weapon, required just as much physical endurance. Consoling himself with the thought that the whole country would know all about it in the morning, he was soon sound asleep.

CHAPTER III

A Flank Movement on the Indian Ring

After nine hours of sleep, so deep and unconscious that an earthquake would not have disturbed it, the editor arose. He had some hope, not much (for he knew of the red tape way of doing things in the departments in Washington), that there might come a reply to the dispatch sent to the Secretary of the Interior. For the next four or five days he watched his eastern exchanges to see what effect the telegrams sent out would have on the country. The first that came to hand were the *Chicago Tribune* and *Missouri Republican*. Both took strong ground for the Poncas and denounced the cruelties practised upon them, and following after came the *New York Herald*, *Tribune*, *Sun*, and many others. No word came from Mr. Carl Schurz, who was the man that under the interpretations given to the laws in this boasted "land of the free" could, by a single word, doom these thirty Indians to death and slavery, or set them free. He took from the shelf the Constitution of the United States and read the portions referring to personal liberty with greater interest than ever in his life before, and between the writing of editorials on current affairs made up his mind on a new course of action. He would find out whether the courts regarded an Indian as a man, or simply as a brute, whether he "had any

rights which a white man was bound to respect." He
found himself again contending for exactly the same
principles for which he fought twenty-four years ago,
the equality of all men before the law.

To test the case there must be a lawsuit. But a lawsuit
would cost money. Now, everybody knows that an honest,
genuine newspaper man, never can earn more than a
support for his family. If he has money to spare, it is a
sure sign he has been writing up somebody, or advocating
some project for which he has been paid outside of his
regular salary. A newspaper man in the West is expected
to work fifteen hours a day, get from fifteen to twenty-
five dollars a week for it, and take part of that out in
advertising. However, as he had once routed a battalion
of border ruffians by the exercise of "pure cheek" he determined to endeavor to carry on a lawsuit in the same way.

There was a lawyer in Omaha who had graduated at
the same college that he did, and with whom he was on
the intimate terms of friendship. This lawyer had been
president of the Nebraska constitutional convention, had
a very large practice, was a hard student, and a man
whose opinions commanded respect in the courts and outside. He laid the case before him, and told him he believed
a writ of *habeas corpus* would hold. The lawyer, Hon.
John L. Webster, took the matter under advisement.

The next day when the editor called, Mr. Webster
said:

This is a question of vast importance. A petition for such
a writ must be based upon broad constitutional grounds, and
the principles involved in it underlie all personal liberty. It is
a question of the natural rights of men, such as was discussed
by the fathers and founders of this government. I am not satisfied
that a writ would hold, on account of the peculiar relation of

Indians to the government. They have always been treated as "wards," as incapable of making contracts, etc., but it will do no harm to try. It seems to me that there ought to be power somewhere to stop this inhuman cruelty, and if it does not reside in the courts where shall we find it? My services are at your disposal, but on account of the magnitude of the questions involved I would like to have assistance. If Hon. A. J. Poppleton will assist me, I will go right to work and draw up the papers. I know of no lawyer in these United States, who can handle these underlying, fundamental questions of government and human liberty more ably than he.

The editor started to find Mr. Poppleton. He knew he was considered without a peer in the legal profession in the State, and that as an orator there were few in the whole country who could so entrance an audience.

Mr. Poppleton had just returned from the east. He was given a printed account of the treatment of the Poncas, and the matter left with him. The next day he was called upon, and he said:

I believe you have a good case. I think we can make the writ hold. It is true that these Indians have been held by the courts as "wards of the nation," but this writ was intended for the weak and helpless—for wards and minors. A ward cannot make a contract, but it does not follow from that, that the guardian can imprison, starve or practise inhuman cruelty upon the ward. The courts always have, and always will interfere in such cases. I will undertake this case, and you can inform Mr. Webster that I will give to it close attention and my best efforts.

The form of the petiton was given as careful study as the necessity for haste would permit. The Indians were likely to be started south at any moment. Judge Dundy, before whom the case had to be brought, lived a hundred and fifty miles away. Considerable telegraphing was done to reach him, and find where he would hear the application. After a day or two it was decided he would hear it in Lincoln.

The form of the petition was as follows:

In the District Court of the United States for the District of Nebraska.

Ma-chu-nah-zha (Standing Bear) vs. George Crook, a Brigadier-General of the Army of the United States, and commanding the Department of the Platte.

In the matter of the application of Ma-chu-nah-zha (Standing Bear), etc., for a writ of *habeas corpus*.

To the Honorable Elmer S. Dundy, Judge of the District Court of the United States, for the District of Nebraska.

The petition of Ma-chu-nah-zha (Standing Bear), Ta-zha-but (Buffalo Chip), Shan-gu-e-he-zhe (Yellow Horse), Nu-don-ah-gaz (Cries for War), Wa-the-ha-cuh-she (Long Runner), Wan-chu-dun (Crazy Bear), Me-tha-zhin-ga (Little Duck), Ta-the-ga-da (Buffalo Track), Ka-wig-i-sha (Turtle Grease), Min-i-chuck (Walk-in-the-Mud), Ta-do-mon-e (Walk-in-the-Wind), Me-gah-sin-de (Coon's tail), E-tun-kah (Big Mouth), Wah-thi-ga (Swift), Ta-wau-oo (Buffalo Cow), Ma-shud-da-de (Feather Crazy), Ze-mon-a (Walking Yellow), Oo-moo-ah (Good Provision), Susette Primo, Laura Primo, Ta-nigh-ing-ah (Little Buffalo Woman), Kre-ah-du-wah (Midst-of-the-Eagles), Me-he-da-wah (Midst-of-the-Sun), Za-zi-zi (Yellow Spotted Buffalo), No-zha-zhe (Grown Hair), Wa-gang-wah, Who respectfully show unto your honor, that each and all of them are prisoners unlawfully imprisoned, detained, confined and in custody, and are restrained of their liberty under and by color of the alleged authority of the United States, by George Crook, a Brigadier-General of the Army of the United States, and Commanding the Department of the Platte, and are so imprisoned, detained, confined, and in custody and restrained of their liberty by said George Crook at Fort Omaha, on a military reservation, under the sole and exclusive jurisdiction of the United States, and located within the Territory of the district of Nebraska. That said imprisonment, detention, confinement and restraint by said George Crook as aforesaid are so done by him, under and by virtue of some order or direction of the United States, or some department thereof, and which order or direction is not more particularly known to these complainants whereby they are unable to more particularly set the same forth, save that the complainants are informed and believe that said order or direction is to the effect that these complainants be taken as such prisoners to the Indian Territory.

These complainants further represent that they are Indians, and of the nationality of the Ponca tribe of Indians, but that for a considerable time before, and at the time of their arrest and imprisonment, as herein more fully set forth, they were separated from the Ponca tribe of Indians, and had been and were separated from their tribal relations to said Ponca tribe of Indians and that so many of the said Ponca tribe of Indians as maintain their tribal relations are located in the Indian Territory.

That your complainants at the time of their arrest and imprisonment were lawfully and peacefully residing on the Omaha Reservation, a tract of land set apart by the United States to the Omaha tribe of Indians, and within the territory of the District of Nebraska, and were so residing there by the consent of said Omaha tribe of Indians, and on lands set apart to your complainants by said Omaha tribe of Indians. That your complainants have made great advancements in civilization, and at the time of the arrest and imprisonment of your complainants, some of them were actually engaged in agriculture, and others were making preparations for immediate agricultural labors, and were supporting themselves by their own labors, and no one of these complainants, was receiving or asking support of the government of the United States.

That your complainants were not violating and are not guilty of any violation of any law of the United States, civil or military, or of any treaty of the United States, for which said arrest and imprisonment were made.

That while your complainants were so peacefully and lawfully residing on said Omaha Reservation as aforesaid, they were each and all unlawfully imprisoned, detained, confined, and restrained of their liberty by said George Crook, as such Brigadier-General, commanding the Department of the Platte, and as such prisoners were transported from their said residence at the Omaha Reservation to Fort Omaha, where they are now still unlawfully imprisoned, detained, confined, and restrained of their liberty by said George Crook, as aforesaid.

Wherefore these complainants say that their said imprisonment and detention is wholly illegal, and they demand that a writ of _habeas corpus_ be granted, directed to the said George Crook, a Brigadier-General of the army of the United States, commanding the Department of the Platte, commanding him to have the bodies of (here followed the list of names) before your honor at a time and place therein to be specified, to do and receive what shall then and there be considered by your honor concerning them, together with the time and cause of their detention, and said writ, and that the complainants may then be restored to their liberty.

Ma-chu-nah-zah (Standing Bear), his X mark.
Ta-zha-but (Buffalo Chip), his X mark.
Ma-chu-dun (Crazy Bear), his X mark.
Shan-gu-he-zhe (Yellow Horse), his X mark.
Na-chen-ah-gaz (Cries for War), his X mark.
Wa-the-ha-cuh-she (Long Runner), his X mark.
Me-tha-zhun-ga (Little Duck), his X mark.
Ta-the-ga-da (Buffalo Track), his X mark.

A. J. POPPLETON and JNO. L. WEBSTER,
Atty's for Petitioners.

UNITED STATES OF AMERICA, ⎫
   DISTRICT OF NEBRASKA, ⎬ ss.
      DOUGLAS CO.   ⎭

Ma-chu-nah-zha (Standing Bear), Ta-zha-but (Buffalo Chip), Shan-gu-e-he-zhe (Yellow Horse), Na-dun-ah-gaz (Cries for War), Wa-the-ha-cuh-she (Long Runner), Wan-chu-dun (Crazy Bear), Ma-the-zhin-ga (Little Duck), Ta-the-ga-da (Buffalo Track), Ka-wig-i-sha (Turtle Grease), Min-i-chuck (Walk-in-the-Mud), Ta-do-mon-e (Walk-in-the-Wind), Me-gah-sin-de (Coon's Tail), E-tun-ka (Big Mouth), Wa-thi-ga (Swift), Ta-wan-oo (Buffalo Cow), Me-shud-da-de (Feather Crazy), Ze-on-a (Walking Yellow), Oo-moo-ah (Good Provision), Susette Primo, Laura Primo, Ta-nigh-ing-ah (Little Buffalo Woman), Kre-ah-du-wah (Midst-of-the-Eagles), Me-he-da-wah (Midst-of-the-Sun), Za-zi-zi (Yellow Spotted Buffalo), No-zha-zhe (Grown Hair), and Wa-gang-wah, being first duly severally sworn according to law, say the facts stated in the foregoing complaint are true.

Ma-chu-nah-zha (Standing Bear), his X mark.

Ta-zha-but (Buffalo Chip), his X mark.

Na-dun-ah-gaz (Cries for War), his X mark.

Shan-gu-he-zhe (Yellow Horse), his X mark.

Ma-chu-dun (Crazy Bear), his X mark.

Ma-the-zhin-ga (Little Duck), his X mark.

Wa-the-ha-cuh-she (Long Runner), his X mark.

Ta-the-ga-da (Buffalo Track), his X mark.

Witnesses.

T. H. TIBBLES, W. L. CARPENTER, U.S.A.

Subscribed in my presence, and sworn to before me, this the 4th day of April, A.D. 1879.

HOMER STULL, *Notary Public.*

[RETURN.]

To the Hon. Elmer S. Dundy, U. S. District Judge, for the District of Nebraska, —

As directed by your writ of *habeas corpus,* dated April 8, 1879, requiring me to take and have the bodies (list of names) by me "imprisoned and detained as it is said, together with the time and cause of such imprisonment, and such detention within ten days after the service" thereof, and to do and receive what shall then and there be considered concerning the said persons, and to have then and there said writ; I have the honor respectfully to state and return in obedience to, and with the said writ, that the bodies of the aforesaid persons are as required produced.

That the time of their detention at Fort Omaha, Neb., is from the 27th of March, 1879, as appears by the report of the commanding officer at that Fort; copy of which and of the special order therefor, is hereto attached and made part of this return, with like effect as though fully set forth herein; that I am the Brigadier-General U. S. A. commanding the Military Department of the Platte, and all officers and soldiers stationed therein, and as such commanding officer, subject to the orders of my military superiors.

That the cause of the detention of aforenamed Indians is the request of the Secretary of the Interior, and the orders of my commanding officers, General Sherman and Lieutenant-General Sheridan, based thereon.

Which orders were to me communicated and directed by the first and second endorsements on the copy of the letter of Hon. C. Schurz, Secretary of the Department of the Interior, dated March 7, 1879, and addressed to the Secretary of War, enclosing a copy of a telegram, dated March 4th, 1879, addressed to the Commissioner of Indian Affairs at Washington, D. C., and signed Jacob Vore, Indian Agent, copies of which letters and telegrams and of said indorsements, are also hereto attached and made part of this return, with like effect as though fully set forth herein, whereby it appears that the Hon. Secretary of the Interior requested the Secretary of War "that the nearest military commander (to the Omaha Indian Agency) may be instructed to detail a sufficient guard to return these Poncas where they belong."

Wherefore the undersigned asks to be released from said writ, and that said Indians may be returned to him for the fulfilment of his orders concerning them.

GEORGE CROOK, *Brigadier-General,*
Commanding Department of the Platte.

STATE OF NEBRASKA, ⎱
COUNTY OF DOUGLAS. ⎰ ss.

Personally appeared before me, Brigadier-General George Crook, U. S. Army, who, being duly sworn according to law, deposes and says that the statements made in the foregoing return are true so far as they are within his own knowledge, and as he is officially informed and believes, of such facts as are stated as based on official information.

GEORGE CROOK, *Brigadier-General U. S. Army.*
Sworn and subscribed this 11th day of April, 1879, before me.

[Seal.]   WM. K. BOWEN, *Notary Public.*

[COPY.]

HEADQUARTERS FORT OMAHA, NEB., ⎱
MARCH 26TH, 1879.   ⎰

To the Assistant Adjutant General, Department of the Platte,
Fort Omaha, Neb.—

SIR, —In pursuance of instructions of the 19th inst., from department headquarters, I have the honor to report the arrival at this post on the 27th inst., from the Omaha Indian Agency, of twenty-six Ponca Indians, consisting of eight men, seven women, and eleven children. Several of the Indians are sick with chills and fever, and it will be necessary for the entire party to remain here for a few days so that their ponies may recuperate sufficiently to enable them to proceed on their return to the Indian Territory. I am, sir, very respectfully, your obedient servant,

(Signed.)   JNO. H. KING,
                    Col. 9th Infantry, Commanding.
Official copy.

R. WILLIAMS, *Ass't Adj't General.*

[COPY.]

HEADQUARTERS FORT OMAHA, NEB., }
MARCH 20, 1879.   }

Special orders, No. 33.

In obedience to instructions from headquarters, Department of the Platte, of the 19th inst., First Lieut. W. L. Carpenter, 9th Infantry, with a guard consisting of   *   *   *   *   *   *   *   will proceed without delay to the Omaha Indian Agency, Neb. Upon arrival thereat, Lieut. Carpenter will call upon the agent in charge for the thirty Ponca Indians who are reported to have recently arrived at that Agency from the Indian Territory.

Upon receiving these Indians Lieut. Carpenter and the guard will bring them to this post.

The quartermaster's department will furnish the necessary transportation, consisting of one four mule team and three saddle horses.

*   *   *   *   *   *   *   *

By order of COL. JOHN H. KING, *9th Infantry.*
(Signed.)   J. M. LEE.
First Lieut. and Adj't, 9th Inf'y, Post Headquarters, Dept. of the Platte.

ASS'T ADJ'T GENL'S OFFICE, }
FORT OMAHA, NEB., April 11th, 1879. }

Official Copy.

R. WILLIAMS, *Ass't Adj't General.*

[COPY.]

DEPARTMENT OF THE INTERIOR, }
WASHINGTON, March 7th, 1879. }

The Honorable, the Secretary of War:

SIR,—I have the honor to transmit herewith a copy of a telegram, dated Omaha, Neb., March 4th, 1879, addressed to the Commissioner of Indian Affairs by Jacob Vore, U. S. Indian Agent at Omaha Agency, Neb., and by the Commissioner referred to this department, with the information that thirty Ponca Indians who have left their agency in the Indian Territory without permission have just arrived at the first named Agency.

In accordance with the desire of the Commissioner, I respectfully request that the nearest military commander may be instructed to detail a sufficient guard to return these Poncas to the Agency where they belong.　　　Very respectfully,

(S. D.)　　　　　　　　　　　C. SCHURZ, *Secretary.*

A true copy.

H. B. BURNHAM, *Judge Advocate, U. S. A.*

[COPY TELEGRAM.]

OMAHA, NEB., March 4th, 1879.

To the Commissioner of Indian Affairs, Washington, D. C.

The Poncas have just arrived, thirty in number; had them arrested; they promise to remain for orders; have no place to confine them. I await instructions.

(S. D.)　　　　　　　　　　JACOB VORE, *Indian Agent.*

A true copy.

H. B. BURNHAM, *Judge Advocate, U. S. A.*

Endorsements on copy of letter of the Secretary of the Interior dated March 7th, 1879, to the Secretary of War, transmitting copy of telegram from Jacob Vore, Indian Agent, Omaha Agency, of March 4th, 1879, stating that thirty Ponca Indians have just arrived at that Agency from Indian Territory, and requests detail of a guard to return them to their Agency.

Official copy referred by General Sherman, March 14th, 1879, to Lieut.-General P. H. Sheridan, Com'g. Mil. Div. of Mo., to comply with the request of the Interior Department.

Referred by Lieut.-General Sheridan, March 17th, 1879, to the Com'g General Department of the Platte for action.

HEADQUARTERS DEP'T OF THE PLATTE,　⎫
ASS'T ADJ'T GEN'L'S OFFICE,　⎬
FORT OMAHA, NEB., March 19.　⎭

Respectfully referred to the commanding officer Fort Omaha, Neb., who will please detail an officer and a guard of enlisted men, to proceed to the Omaha Agency, and return the Indians to their Agency in the Indian Territory, as directed by the General of the Army. If the Indians referred to came mounted, as they probably did, they will go back in the same manner, and in this event it will be necessary to provide horses for the detachment of troops returning with them.

By command of BRIGADIER-GEN'L. CROOK.

(Signed)   R. WILLIAMS.

UNITED STATES OF AMERICA, ⎫ ss.
  DISTRICT OF NEBRASKA.   ⎭

I, Watson B. Smith, clerk of the District Court of the U. S., for the District of Nebraska, certify that I have compared the annexed copy of return, in case of U. S. ex rel. Ma-chu-nah-zah (Standing Bear), et al., vs. George Crook, Brigadier-General, etc., with the original on file in this office, and that the same is a correct transcript thereof, and of the whole of said original.

In testimony whereof I have caused the seal of said court to be affixed, at the city of Omaha, in said District, this 25th day of April, 1879.

(Seal)   WATSON B. SMITH, *Clerk*.

By the consent of court, and agreement of parties, the following amendment was inserted in the body of the return:

That the said complainant, Standing Bear, is an Indian Chief of the Ponca tribe of Indians; that the other petitioners are members of said tribe of Ponca Indians; that said complainants have not dissolved, but still retain their tribal relations with said tribe of Ponca Indians, and pay allegiance to the tribal head of said Ponca tribe of Indians; that said complainants have not adopted and are not pursuing the habits and vocations of civilized life; that these complainants are not illegally restrained of their liberty, but were arrested on the Omaha reservation, where they were in violation of law, and were arrested in pursuance of the authority hereinafter set forth for the purpose of returning them to the Indian agency and reservation where they belong, located in the Indian Territory.

This being inserted in the body of the return, appeared on the record over the signature of Gen. Crook. To this, through the Judge Advocate of his department, Col. Burnham, he protested. He did not wish his name signed to any such document, or statement, and he had never authorized any one to sign it for him.

The court explained that he was not signing it as Gen. Crook, personally, but as a Brigadier-General of the Army, and for the Government. Gen. Crook continued to protest, and Judge Dundy explained again. The General never did give his consent that his name should go to it, and yet that is the way it appears on the records of the court. Such are some of the ways of the law, and yet Gen. Crook no doubt to this day cannot see why it was necessary for him to sign a statement which was not true.*

*[The amended return was filed on the second and concluding day of the trial, and in his write-up of the case for the May 4 *Daily Herald* Tibbles gave a similar account of Crook's protest in court.

The text of the petition and return as originally printed in *The Ponca Chiefs* differs slightly from the court documents themselves. The wording has been silently corrected above to correspond to the court record (see the Note on the Text, p. 139).—*ed. note*]

CHAPTER IV

Mr. Hayt's Assault on Standing Bear, and the Reply the Old Chief Made

During the ten days intervening before the trial, several things happened worthy of record. Commissioner Hayt published the following letter:

WASHINGTON, D.C., April 10th, 1879.
The Honorable the Secretary of the Interior:—

SIR,—I have the honor to forward herewith a brief statement of facts regarding the Ponca Indians, who recently went from the Indian Territory to Nebraska. By the treaty of 1868 the Sioux were given lands in Dakota to the east bank of the Missouri River, which included the Ponca reservation. As the Poncas and Sioux had been at feud for many years previous, it became necessary to remove the Poncas from their reservation to save them from the destruction that would be likely to overtake them from the location of the Sioux on the Missouri River. By the Indian Appropriation acts of August 15, 1876, and March 3, 1877, Congress provided for the removal of the Poncas to the Indian Territory, and in pursuance thereof they had to be so removed, and were located on the Quapaw reservation. They, however, expressed great dissatisfaction with the place to which they had been sent, and undoubtedly with good reason, and upon their request they were permitted to send a large representation to Washington to make known to the President and to the department their grievances and wishes. There being no way by which their request to be sent back North could be complied with without action of Congress in the matter, they were permitted to make their own selection among the best lands in the Indian Territory. A delegation of chiefs was accordingly sent with an Indian inspector, and, after a careful examination of various points, they selected an eligible location at the junction of the Salt Fork and the Arkansas River. There is probably no finer location for an Indian settlement in the Indian Territory, and in all respects it is far superior to their old location in Dakota, from which, in previous years, they had themselves asked the department to remove them.

I visited these Indians during the month of October last, and found their condition very much improved, both as to their outward circumstances and their feelings. Every effort was made, and large sums of money were expended to provide for their comfort, and they received a sawmill, timber and all appliances for building houses, as well as an abundant supply of cattle and agricultural implements, and they entered upon the work with a good deal of determination, and are undoubtedly succeeding as well as any Indians could under the most favorable circumstances. It is true that during the first four months of their residence in the Indian Territory they lost a large number by death, which is inevitable in all cases of removal of Northern Indians to a Southern latitude. They have, however, been in the Indian Territory long enough to become acclimated. Their sanitary condition is vastly improved, and henceforward they may expect to have as good health as they would in any other location.

During my visit to the Agency above referred to I ascertained that Standing Bear was dissatisfied, but that he was the only one among the chiefs who showed a bad spirit. He was constantly grumbling, and held aloof from the other chiefs, and seemed full of discontent, which he took no pains to conceal, while the other Poncas were at work. The agent informed me that he expected that Standing Bear would leave the Agency at the first favorable opportunity. It was not thought expedient at that time to put him in confinement, as one chief out of ten or twelve was hardly of sufficient importance to deal with in that manner. Soon afterward he made his escape, and at the present time, as may be judged from current reports, endeavors to attract public sympathy by grossly misrepresenting the circumstances of the case. The removal of Northern Indians to the Indian Territory was probably not good policy, but it was done in pursuance of laws enacted before the present administration came into power.

There is no law at present for moving these Indians back to their old reservation or to any other place. If the reservation system is to be maintained, discontented and restless or mischievous Indians cannot be permitted to leave their reservation at will and go where they please. If this were permitted the most necessary discipline of the reservations would soon be entirely broken up, all authority over the Indians would cease, and in a short time the Western country would swarm with roving and lawless bands of Indians, spreading a spirit of uneasiness and restlessness even among those Indians who are now at work and doing well. The government should be, and undoubtedly is, willing to redress all their real grievances as far as they can be redressed; but it must, in my opinion, be done in such a way as not to subvert all control over the Indians, or to put all arrangements made in pursuance of law and with large expenditures of money at the mercy of the caprice of mischievous individuals or bands among the Indian tribes. The task of transforming the nomadic habits of Indians into habits of permanent settlement and steady and self-supporting work, is a very difficult one at best, requiring the introduction and maintenance of certain rules of discipline which cannot be enforced in every case without sometimes producing individual hardships, and which cannot be abandoned without detriment to the best interests of the large majority of our Indian wards.

I have the honor to be, sir, very respectfully, your obedient servant.   E. A. HAYT, *Commissioner.*

This letter was shown to Standing Bear, and he made the following reply:

The Commissioner says our lands were given to the Sioux. Who had any authority to give our lands to the Sioux? The land belonged to us, and not to the Commissioner or General Sherman. What right had he to give it to the Sioux? The Ponca tribe was never informed of any such transaction, and never agreed to do anything of the kind. What would the Commissioner think if some man should give his land to the Sioux. He says we are not sick any more in the Indian Territory. I will only point you to these lodges. There are now seven very sick people in them, out of this small party. The army doctor who is attending to them will tell you how sick they are, and that they caught their sickness down there. Seven persons out of thirty very sick, and five or six others not well enough to work, proves that the Commissioner's words are not true. There is the same proportion of sick in all the tribe. The Commissioner says I show a bad spirit! He must have changed his mind about me. I will show you a paper signed by his own name, and you can judge whether he told the truth then, or whether he tells it now.

Standing Bear then went to a trunk and took out a large roll of papers. Among them was the following:

DEPARTMENT OF THE INTERIOR,
OFFICE OF INDIAN AFFAIRS,
WASHINGTON, D.C., Dec. 18th, 1877.

This is to certify that Standing Bear is a chief of the Ponca Indians. This tribe is at peace with the United States, and Standing Bear is recognized as a chief of said tribe, whose influence has been to preserve peace and harmony between the Ponca Indians and the United States, and as such is entitled to the confidence of all persons whom he may meet.   *   *   *   *
(Seal.)   E. A. HAYT, *Commissioner.*

It was remarked that "Mr. Hayt *gave* him a good character." Standing Bear did not seem to understand, for he replied, "The Commissioner did not give me a good character. I got my character by a long life devoted to the advancement of my tribe. Many years before other white men have said the same about me. They could not say differently if they told the truth." He then showed the following documents:

To whom it may concern:

This is to certify that Standing Bear, the bearer hereof, is an Indian, full blood, of the Ponca tribe, and a chief of said tribe. He is a reliable and trustworthy man, of industrious habits, and rare zeal in setting a good example to the Indians and inciting them to industrious and civilized habits. He and his wife are one in the good work of providing comfortably for their home and children, who are likewise taught to work and respect all who do. If the Poncas had no other councilors but such men as Standing Bear, their condition would not long be one of helpless dependence. I most heartily commend him to the kindness of all to whom he may present this.

A. J. CARRIER, *U.S. Indian Agent.*

Ponca Agency, D. T., March 30th, 1876.

To all whom this may come:

The bearer, Ma-chu-na-zha (Standing Bear), is one of the head chiefs of the Ponca tribe of Indians. He is civil, quiet and well-behaved, a warm friend of the whites, and loyal to the government. He is deserving of respect and kind treatment from all to whom he may present himself whenever traveling through the settlements.

WM. H. HUGO, *First Lieutenant, U.S. Army.*

Standing Bear exhibited a large number of these documents, all speaking of him in the very highest terms, some of them dating back as far as 1865. After they were examined Standing Bear remarked: "You see that the Commissioner did not *give* me my character; he only certified to what was true."

The translation of the letter was continued, and that part was read where Mr. Hayt says: "There being no way whereby their request to be sent back North could be complied with," Standing Bear smiled and said: "No one asked the Commissioner to *send* me back North. All I wanted was permission to come. Now I am already North, and that difficulty is overcome. If the Commissioner can't send me North, he seems to know of a very quick way to send me South."

Coming to that part where Mr. Hayt says "large sums were expended," Standing Bear said, "That may be so, but all the money we ever got was $6.25 a head. There was a good deal of money at the Agency. I know that we never got it. Besides I don't want the Commissioner's money. All I ask is to be allowed to make my own living. I can take care of myself if they don't keep me under arrest. The statement of a supply of cattle and agricultural implements is untrue."

In regard to the disaffections of other chiefs against Standing Bear, he said:

In every tribe of Indians there are two parties. First, those who understand that it is necessary, if the Indians are not all to be exterminated, to go to work, to learn to read and write and count money, to be like white men. Those who think about these things at all, know that the game is all gone, and that our mode of life must change. Then there are always some who believe in the old traditions, who think the Great Spirit will be displeased with them if they do like white men. They want to retain their old habits and religion. They hate to work. They want to lie in the shade in the summer, and near the fire in the winter, and make their women wait on them. These two classes gather around the chiefs who represent these two things. There are a few of these Indians who do not want to work among the Poncas. They have a chief, and he don't like me, because I tell him and his band that they are not good Indians, and if the tribe should follow his advice there would soon be not one Ponca left to tell what had become of us. The bad agents, half-breeds, and all those who make their living from the money which is sent to tribes which are not advanced enough to make their own living, give a great deal of encouragement to this sort of Indians, and pretend that they have a great deal more influence than they really have. I represent in the Ponca tribe the foremost of those who want to support themselves, to send their children to school, to build houses, to get property and all kinds of stock around us, and to be independent. It may be that those lazy, bad Indians told the Commissioner that I had no influence. They would do so if they had a chance. But if I could go down to the Territory, and tell all the tribe to follow me who wanted to work and send their children to school, nine out of every ten would come with me. A few would object, but there are not more than fifteen or twenty of them. White Eagle thinks the same way about these matters that I do. He is a good man, and has great influence in the tribe. The Commissioner may have intended no wrong to me in making the statement. He may have been so informed, but if he had issued an order for my arrest he would soon have learned whether I had friends in the tribe or not. There might have been trouble, for I could not have been with them to have told them what to do. My voice has always been for peace. Some others have advised differently.

CHAPTER V

The Omahas Come to
Standing Bear's Aid

The next day after this conversation, the following petition from the Omaha tribe was received. The petition was drawn up and forwarded by Chas. P. Morgan, who is a full-blooded Omaha.

OMAHA AGENCY, April 21, 1879.
To the friends of the Poncas now held as prisoners at Omaha barracks:

We, the undersigned, Omaha Indians, for ourselves, and on behalf of the Omaha tribe, wish publicly to declare that in consideration of the relationship existing between our tribe and those Poncas, and under a sense of the dictates of common humanity to our race, we are anxious for their return to our reservation, and are willing to share with them our lands, and to assist them until they can, by their industry, support themselves. They are our brothers and our sisters, our uncles and our cousins, and although we are called savages we feel that sympathy for our persecuted brethren that should characterize Christians, and are willing to share what we possess with them if they can only be allowed to return and labor, improve and provide for themselves where they may live in peace, enjoy good health, and the opportunity of educating their children up to a higher state of civilization. They came here to our reservation about the first of March, from the Indian Territory, and as they believe from the jaws of death, even bringing sickness with them. We received them kindly and hospitably, and afforded them such assistance as we could in the way of land to raise a crop this summer, and they were preparing to go to work to sow and plant when they were arrested and taken from us by soldiers without any just cause or provocation that we or they know of. Having learned with thankfulness that the good people of Omaha, and the friends of humanity and justice deeply sympathized with and enlisted in the cause of these Poncas, we feel encouraged to appeal to you for a continuance of your efforts in their behalf, until their right to live among their friends and brothers and enjoy the fruits of their labor is restored to them.

Fire-Chief,	Standing Hawk,
Yellow Smoke,	Hard-Walker,
Ga-he-ga,	Shon-ga-skah,
Paw-nee-num-puzzhe	Du-ba-mo-ni,
Ta-o-ka-hah,	Um-pa-tun-ga,
Wah-ha-wa-ne,	Mo-wad-da-na,
Num-ba-du-ba,	Hog-ga-mo-ni,
Gah-ke-a-mo-ni,	Wah-jap-pa,
Wah-ke-da,	Nah-ha-wa-kah,
Mah-pe-a-hog-ga,	Ta-noo-ga.

The *New York Herald* made the following comment upon this petition:

The appeal of the Omaha Indians in favor of their kindred, the Poncas, is one of the most extraordinary statements ever published in America. Whether some portion of it may not be the work of a white man we are not prepared to deny; but the facts are of more consequence than the rhetoric, and these are simply that a tribe of Indians, nominally civilized, but still savage in the estimation of many whites, are willing and anxious to recieve the Poncas on their reservation, allot lands to them, and assist them until they can make crops and support themselves. Many white men in Nebraska might have made the same offer without hurting themselves, and the news of such a deed would have gone through the entire Indian country with benefit to the dominant race. But white men did not do it. Church members talked and petitioned, but not an acre of land did they offer. It was reserved for a band of heathen redskins, who have hardly yet forgotten the war-whoop, to emphasize that sympathy which civilization and religion have talked about—and only talked. The world moves, but civilization seems sometimes to stand still, while savages pass to the front and into the position of honor.

Rev. J. Owen Dorsey, who is engaged in linguistic labors, preserving various Indian languages, was at the Omaha Agency the day the Poncas were arrested. Long Runner refused to obey the order to go. He was surrounded and a gun was placed at his head. He told them to kill him there, for he would rather die than go back. He was tied and a guard placed over him. Word was sent to the others to report and be ready to start at noon.

Mr. Dorsey wrote a letter to Col. Meacham, editor of *The Council Fire*, who was at the time in Washington, in which he said:

I saw them leave to-day. All but the prisoner (Long Runner) went about half a mile in advance of the soldiers without a guard and without a struggle, save that *which was going on in their own hearts*. Their appeals to me were touching. Said Standing Bear: "My friend, you know us. We can't live down there where the Great Father put us. So we came here to live and work the land."

Mr. Dorsey asked Col. Meacham to see the Secretary of the Interior and Commissioner and appeal to them in Standing Bear's behalf. Col. Meacham made the following report of his interview with them:

They gave me a patient hearing. I read your (Rev. Mr. Dorsey's) letter to them a second time. Mr. Schurz remarked:

"That is a sad case. I feel deeply for the Poncas. They are peaceable and quiet, and I wish I could better their condition."

Mr. Hayt—"There is no use of talking about the Poncas going North. They must remain where they are. We have expended large sums of money for them in their new home. They have become acclimated (*sic!!*). They are there by law(?). They cannot be sent North without authority of Congress. They must stay where they are. Those who have left must be taken back. If we allow them to stay away the others will follow."

Col. Meacham—"If a mistake has been made, *we* made it. The Indian was in our power. He was helpless, and is still helpless. He is at our mercy. *He* should not pay the penalty of *our* mistakes. We have it in our power to relieve him of the wrong. True, we cannot call back the dead, but we can do justice to the living. *Let us do right because it is right.*"

Mr. Hayt—"Right is for the Poncas to stay where we have placed them. If we suffer them to leave their homes, the Pawnees, and Cheyennes and Nez Perces must go next. We cannot do that. *It was a mistake to give the Sioux the Ponca country.* This mistake was made by Gen. Sherman before our administration began. I am sure Congress will not consent to send all these Indians back North. We must reconcile them to stay where they are in the Indian Territory."

Col. Meacham—"Gentlemen, I submit that there is a principle involved in this matter. I doubt the right of any man to say that another man shall not live where God placed him. If the Pawnees, Poncas and Nez Perces cannot live in the Indian Territory we ought to move them out."

Col. Meacham closes his report of this interview with these words:

The Commissioner insisted that the Poncas must return. I will make another effort. Ever yours, for God's children,

A. B. MEACHAM.*

*Note:—Mr. Meacham afterward visited the Poncas in the Indian Territory and made reports which greatly injured their cause.

[Alfred B. Meacham, a long-time employee of the Indian Bureau and editor of the Indian-rights publication *Council Fire*, traveled to the Ponca reservation in July, 1879, as a government paymaster. After an apparently superficial inspection, he sent Schurz an unrealistically glowing report of the Poncas' improved condition (Stanley Clark, "Ponca Publicity," *Mississippi Valley Historical Review* 29 [March 1943]: 503).—*ed. note*]

CHAPTER VI

The Omahas Frightened at the Claims of the Commissioner

When the letter of Commissioner Hayt was published, the educated Omahas were frightened, because it claimed absolute power over their bodies, to remove them anywhere, at the will of the Commissioner, and one of them wrote a letter to Omaha, inquiring if the Commissioner, just because she was an Indian, could order her to the Indian Territory, New Mexico, or any place he pleased, and she could not appeal to the law for protection. She stated that if it was true, rather than live in constant dread of such a fate, she would go to Canada and live under the protection of the British government, where this Commissioner could not lay his hands on her. She was informed that the object of this suit was to ascertain that very thing.

Actuated by a similar feeling, another Indian girl prepared a statement concerning the Poncas, which she proposed to publish. Not knowing the nature of the document, she was requested through Mr. Dorsey to forward it to the editor, that it might be submitted to counsel. The following is a *verbatim* copy of her letter and the statement which she prepared, excepting the blank for the name:

OMAHA AGENCY, April 29th, 1879

MR. _____ , DEAR SIR.—Mr. Dorsey requested me to send you the inclosed copy of a statement made by the Ponca chiefs at my house on their return from the Indian Territory about two years ago. We had it published at their desire in one of the Sioux City papers at the time, and I kept the original, thinking it might be of use at some future time. I send also the telegram which the chiefs sent to Washington about the same time. On reaching their home after leaving here, they were ordered to get ready to go to the Indian Territory, and soldiers were sent to them to force them to go. I feel a deep interest in the subject, as White Swan, one of the chiefs who was taken down, is my uncle. My father and I went to Columbus to bid him and his family good-bye on their way down, and the soldiers were with them there. My uncle says they never signed any paper, petition, or treaty to be taken down to Indian Territory, although it is said a petition signed with their names was seen in Washington. The chiefs told us that when the white men were trying to make them sign the paper, they were asked to allow the Ponca tribe to live with the Omahas. They, the white men, told the chiefs, "No, the Omahas are to be taken down too." The chiefs then asked to be allowed to live with the Sioux and mingle with them as one people; that the two tribes were formerly enemies, but they had made peace with them and would rather live with them than be sent to Indian Territory. This also was denied them, and they were told to get ready to go.

The statement shows how much they trusted in the justice of the white people, believing that the wrong done them had been done only by a few, and without authority. I do hope some action will be taken in the matter soon.   Yours respectfully,

BRIGHT EYES.

STATEMENT OF PONCA CHIEFS

We, the Ponca chiefs and principal men of the tribe, desire to make the following statement of facts concerning ourselves in all good faith, hoping it may come to the ears of the President of the United States, whom we are glad to learn is a good man and anxious to do justice to all.

Some time ago there came a man to our reserve, who said he was sent by the Great Father at Washington to make a treaty with us for our land. We said the President was our friend, and this was our home, but we would hear what he had to say. If he wanted our land we would go to Washington and talk about it. He told us he was ordered to do what he did, seemed sincere and friendly, and to satisfy us he sent a telegram to Washington, and after getting an answer, he said he would take ten of our chiefs to see the Indian Territory, where we could select a new home, and that the money for our present journey would be furnished from the Sioux's funds.

We got ready and started, wishing first to visit the Omaha reserve, but this was not allowed us. After some days we reached the country of the Osages, and looked over the country and found it stony and broken, and not a country that we thought we could make a living in. We saw the Osages there, and they were without shirts, their skin burned, and their hair stood up as if it had not been combed since they were little children. We did not wish to sink so low as they seemed to be.

The remainder of the statement is only a repetition of that of Standing Bear, made in the first chapter. The statement is signed by White Eagle, Standing Buffalo, Standing Bear, Smoke Maker, White Swan, Big Elk, and Ga-he-ga.

The following is the telegram which Standing Bear said that he and John Springer sent to the President, and which was also enclosed in the letter of Bright Eyes.

To the President of the United States:

Was it by your authority that the men you sent to take us down to the Indian Territory, to select a home, left us there without money, and without an interpreter or pass, to find our way back as best we could? And did you tell him to say to us: "If you don't select a home here, you shall be driven from your present home at the point of the bayonet?" Please answer, as we are in trouble.

We have been fifty days in getting back as far as the Otoes; tired, hungry, shoeless and footsore, and with heart and spirit broken and sad.

This was signed with the same names as the above statement.

Perhaps it would be well here to refer to the remarks of Gen. Crook, at the close of the council with Standing Bear, when he was first brought to Fort Omaha. After Standing Bear's brief rehearsal of his treatment by the government, Gen. Crook said:

I have heard all this story before. It is just as they represent it. *It has long since been reported to Washington. They have all the facts in Washington,* and it would do no good for me to intercede. I might send a telegram, but it is likely to do more harm than good.

Many who read the report of Gen. Crook's remarks in the papers, thought he was mistaken about the facts being known at Washington, that it was almost beyond belief that the authorities would countenance such treatment of the Indians. These documents show how truthfully he spoke.

CHAPTER VII

Standing Bear's Religion — What Army Officers Think of Him

As much had been said about these Poncas being savages, Standing Bear was asked to state his religious belief. Without a moment's reflection, he spoke as follows:

There is one God, and He made both Indians and white men. We were all made out of the dust of the earth. I once thought differently. I believed there were happy hunting-grounds, where there were plenty of game, and plenty to eat, no sickness, no death, and no pain. The best of the Indians would go to these happy hunting-grounds. I thought that those who were bad would never live any more; that when they died that was the end of them. But I have learned that these things are not so, and that God wishes us to love Him and obey His commandments, follow the narrow road, work for Him on earth, and we shall have happiness after we die. I am told His Son died for us, died that we might live. I want to try and do something for Him, to be like Him, follow in His footsteps as nearly as I can. I think there is but one God. I need help to do right, and I pray to Him that he will help me for His Son's sake. I do not wish to do anything wrong. I wish to follow the narrow road. It is the road of happiness. God never does anything wrong. He knows what is best for me. No man can understand God, or know why He deals with us as He does. Sometimes what we think is the worst is the best for us. When I was arrested by the soldiers and brought down here, I thought for a little while that God had forsaken me, but now I see that, perhaps, it is the best thing for me and my people. If they would only hearken to His word, they would find that all is for their good. He sees me all the time. He watches over me, and knows all I do. He knows my thoughts. He knows when I think wicked thoughts. He knows it all. If He did not watch over me, and take care of me, I should die. I want Him to watch over me, and take care of me, and I believe He always will. He helps me. I can do nothing without His help. I love His truth. I hate lies. I wish to follow the truth always. God has control of the whole earth, and everything is in His power. He sees over all things at once, every man, woman, and child, and knows their thoughts and actions, and everything they do. He watches over me wherever I go. He sees me here to-day. He has been with me through all my wanderings, and has taken care of me. He has seen how I have been taken away from my land. Through all this He has been close to me. When I have felt that I had no friends, I remembered that He was my Father. His people have been good to me, but the people of the devil are trying to send me to hell. They have tried to make me believe that God tells them what to do, as though God would put a man where he would be destroyed, and they have destroyed many already, but they cannot deceive me. God put me here, and intends for me to live on the land they are trying to cheat me out of.

I pray to God every day for Him to help me to regain my rights, if I am worthy of it. For His Son's sake I have asked it. He made me and the whites, and although we are of a different color, I think men's hearts are all alike. If I were to go back to my land to-day, the first thing I would do would be to fall down on my knees and thank God for it. I think in the future, as I grow in years, I will try to love Him more and more every day, do that which is right, and be afraid to do that which is wrong.

He was asked how long he had held these views, and he replied, "Since the missionary came up from Omaha Agency, about eight years ago, and told me the right way."

"How many of the tribe think the same way on this subject that you do?"

"Only a few. It is a hard thing to say, but I will tell you the truth. Some of these have died since we went down to the Territory. We had no missionary down there, and no one to talk to us about God. My boy, who died there, would get a few in a tent and talk to them sometimes and tell them the right way the best he knew how. He used to pray with me very often, and read to me out of the Testament. Some of the people who were sick prayed all the time when they were dying. They asked God to take them away from there if it was His will, or to end their sufferings speedily. When any one came to our old reservation to talk of God, I would always find a place for him to speak, and get the people to come."

AN ARMY OFFICER'S STATEMENT

By request, Lieut. Carpenter, who was detailed to make the arrest of Standing Bear and his party, made the following statement in writing:

On the 23d day of March, 1879, acting under orders of my superior officers, I arrested a band of twenty-nine Ponca Indians, under Standing Bear, at the Omaha Indian Agency, and brought them to Fort Omaha, Neb. At the time of the arrest, while holding a council with the party, Standing Bear made an able speech to me, in which he reviewed the situation of his people, and declared their desire to remain where they were; although consenting under vigorous protest to accompany me. He stated that he had always been a friend to the whites, and that on one occasion he found a poor soldier on the plains in midwinter, with both feet frozen, and nearly starved to death; that he carried him in his arms to camp and took care of him for several weeks until he died. "And now," said he, "you, a soldier, come here to drive me from the land of my fathers."

When arrested they were in a pitiable condition from the effects of chills and fever. Over half of the adults suffered from this disease on the march to Omaha, and, notwithstanding the best medical treatment while prisoners, many are still in feeble health. Before leaving their camp, the women and children cried piteously at the prospect of going back to the Indian Territory. They must have suffered greatly during their winter march, but no charge of depredations while *en route* has ever been made against them.

From my personal knowledge of these people while under my charge, I consider them further advanced in civilization than any other tribe west of the Mississippi, with the single exception of the Omahas, to whom they are related by the bond of common origin. The men are industrious and willing to work, at anything they can find to do. The children conduct themselves well, and the women are modest in their demeanor and neat in appearance and domestic habits.

Fort Omaha, Neb., May 8th, 1879.

By reference to the dates it will be seen that the above statement was written after these Indians had been under Lieut. Carpenter's charge over two months, so that he had had ample opportunities to observe them closely, and know of their character and habits. Every man among them able to work has been at work since their arrival at Fort Omaha, being employed by the contractors on the government buildings. One, who worked a few days, was forced to quit on account of the return of malarial disease.

CHAPTER VIII

Standing Bear's Appeal to the Courts

The case came to trial on the 30th of April, 1879,* and lasted two days, including one evening session. The following chapter contains a *verbatim* report of the evidence:

THE EVIDENCE

Willie W. Hamilton, sworn on behalf of the relators, and examined in chief by Mr. Webster, testified as follows:

Q. You may state your age.

A. Twenty-two.

Q. Where do you live?

A. At the Omaha Agency. That is where I have lived for the last twelve years.

Q. What are you engaged in at the Agency?

A. I have been in a store for the last six years, selling goods.

Q. To what people were you selling goods?

A. The Omaha Indians.

Q. On their reservation?

A. On their reservation, yes, sir.

Q. Are you acquainted with the Omaha language?

A. Yes, sir.

*[See the Note on the Text, p. 140. —*ed. note*]

The Court—Do the Poncas speak the same language?

A. Yes, sir.

Mr. Webster—You are able then to talk with both Omahas and Poncas in their native tongue?

A. Yes, sir.

Q. Do you know the parties that are under arrest at the present time at Omaha?

A. I do.

Q. How long have you known them?

A. I became acquainted with them since they came down here, twenty-two days ago. I saw them when they came to the Agency, but not to talk with them or become acquainted with them.

Q. When was it that they came to the Agency?

A. They came to the Agency in March, I think.

Q. That is last March?

A. Yes, sir, I think it was in the fore part of the month. I won't be certain.

Q. Where does your father live?

A. My father lives at the Agency, or about three miles from the Agency.

Q. How long has he been living there?

A. For the same length of time I have—twelve years.

Q. What has been his business?

A. He is a missionary to the Indians.

Q. How long has he been such?

A. He has been missionary among the Iowas and Omahas for over thirty years.

Q. State the condition of these Poncas when they arrived at the Omaha Agency, so far as you observed?

A. So far as I know they were in a very bad condition when they came there.

Q. What property did they have when they came there?

A. All they had was their horses and wagons and tents.

Q. How were they supplied as to clothing?

A. They had blankets, some of them, and some had coats; those that had coats wore pants, and were dressed in citizens' clothes.

Q. Do you know where they came from when they arrived at the Agency?

A. They said they came from the Indian Territory.

Q. Do you know how they came up from the Indian Territory to the Agency?

A. They came up in wagons, some of them horseback, and others on foot.

Q. State the number that came.

A. I don't know exactly the number that came—I think about thirty-five.

Q. How many were men, about the number approximately, and how many were women, and how many were children?

A. Ten or twelve were men, I think. I don't know how many were children, or how many were women. I was not among them much at first, and I did not pay any attention to them. I think there must have been between twelve and fifteen women.

Q. You may state whether or not they were divided into families at the time when they came—whether they were married and composed families as man and wife?

A. They were.

Q. And the children were the children of these families?

A. Yes, sir, some of them—some were orphans, living with their relations.

Q. Which ones do you speak of as being orphans?

A. There were two orphans came with them. There is

one (indicating a young Indian boy who was present with the relators in the court room) sitting in the woman's lap. The other is at camp.

Q. Whose son is this one here?

A. He is a grandson of Standing Bear's.

Q. Which one is Standing Bear?

A. That one in the corner (indicating one of the three Indian men present.)

Q. Who is this woman who sits here?

A. She is the wife of Standing Bear.

Q. The child is the grandson of Standing Bear and this woman?

A. Yes, sir.

Q. What is her name?

A. Susette.

Q. Is the father of that child living or dead?

A. Dead.

Q. And the other orphan that you speak of, what relation does it sustain to Standing Bear and Susette?

A. Grand-daughter.

[Objected to by counsel for the government as immaterial, and not tending to show that these Indians have dissolved their tribal relations.]

Mr. Webster—Tell us who is that man sitting next to Standing Bear?

A. Yellow Horse.

Q. Do you know what relation he is to Standing Bear?

[Objected to by counsel for government as incompetent. Overruled.]

A. They are brothers.

Q. State what these Indians were engaged in after they arrived at the Omaha Agency?

A. What little time they staid there they were engaged in helping the Omahas put in their crops.

Q. What crops were the Omahas putting in?

A. Wheat.

Q. State what one, if any, of the Indians, the Poncas, were putting in crops for themselves?

A. Buffalo Chip was helping put in a crop for himself. His friends at the Omaha Agency gave him land enough to sow his wheat.

Q. At the time of the arrest, state, if you know, about the amount of wheat Buffalo Chip had put in on this land which was set apart for him?

A. I think there must have been four or five acres sowed.

Q. You may state what the habits of the Omahas were at the Agency where these Indians were, as to labor and agriculture?

A. They are all, or the greater part of them, on their farms. They have a great deal of land broken, and each one has his farm to himself.

Q. State whether the land is allotted to the members of the tribe?

A. It is.

Q. State what day of the week it was when these Indians were arrested?

A. It was on Sunday.

Q. On that day, state whether they were resting from their labors?

A. They were.

Q. State whether it is the habit of the Poncas to rest on the Sabbath day from their labor?

The Court—Is that necessary?

Mr. Webster—The theory of this goverment is to Christianize these Indians, I believe.

The Witness—It is about the same as it is with white men, some do, and some do not.

Mr. Webster—State how many of these Poncas, during their stay at the Omaha Agency, were engaged in labor—whether all were so engaged?

A. All that were able to were.

Q. Those who were not employed in actual labor, state why they were not?

[Objected to as immaterial by counsel for the government. Objection overruled.]

Mr. Webster—You may answer why the others were not engaged in labor.

A. Because they were sick and unable to work.

Q. How many of their number were sick when they arrived on the Agency and unable to work?

A. There were hardly any of them able to work when they arrived on the Agency—not more than one or two, so far as I could learn.

Q. During their stay at the Agency, and prior to their arrest by Lieut. Carpenter, state to what extent they had improved in health so as to be able to commence labor?

A. They had improved a good deal, but those who were working were not really able to work.

Q. At the time of their arrest by Lieut. Carpenter about how many had begun to labor?

A. I think five or six out of the twelve.

Q. State whether any are engaged in labor now at the Fort?

[Objected to by counsel for government. Objection sustained.]

CROSS-EXAMINED

Dist.-Att'y Lambertson—How many Indians came there?

A. Thirty-five I think. I don't know the exact number.

The Court—How many join in the petition—twenty-seven?

Mr. Lambertson—I believe there are not quite that many. The children, I think, are not put in the petition. (*To the witness.*) At the time they were arrested, five or six were engaged in agricultural pursuits?

A. Yes, sir.

Q. Were they squaws?

A. No, sir.

Q. Standing Bear was working, was he?

A. Yes, sir.

Q. Then there were five of the thirty-five that were working?

A. Only that many in the field. The women were working around their tents. They are not supposed to go into the fields.

Q. Who was their chief?

A. Standing Bear is the head chief of the tribe. Buffalo Chip was the chief of these Indians here. Standing Bear has a tribe of about a hundred, I think; I do not know the exact number.

Q. You don't know what some of them, or a good many of them did at the Indian Territory before they arrived at the Omaha Agency?

A. I know that a good many of them died before he left with his tribe.

Q. And the original number of his tribe was about a hundred?

A. Yes, sir.

Q. He was their acknowledged chief there at the Agency?

A. Yes, sir.

Q. Did they obey his orders?

A. Yes, sir.

Q. What other chiefs have they?

A. There are several chiefs down at the lower Agency in the Indian Territory. I was not there.

Q. Name some of the other chiefs that were arrested.

A. Standing Bear, Buffalo Chip, and Chicken Hunter.

Q. These managed and controlled the Indians?

A. Yes, sir. Each one controlled his own band.

Q. They lived at the Omaha Agency as the friends of the Omaha Indians?

A. Yes, sir; while they were there.

Q. They followed the same pursuit the other Indians did?

A. Yes, sir.

Q. What did they live in—tents?

A. Yes, sir; they brought their tents, I think.

Q. These tents were provided by the government?

A. These tents were made by themselves.

Q. These wagons were furnished by the government?

A. Yes, sir; they brought their wagons with them.

Q. Did they have any citizens' clothes?

A. They had.

Q. These clothes were also provided by the government?

A. Yes, sir; some were, and some were not.

Q. Some of them wore blankets?

A. Some wore blankets, pants, and vests, and some wore Indian clothes throughout.

Q. These blankets—were they provided by the government?

A. Some of them—yes, sir.

Q. You say Standing Bear had put in about five acres of wheat?

A. No, sir; Buffalo Chip had. There was three or four acres put in for Standing Bear by the police of the Omahas.

Q. Then Standing Bear didn't put in any himself?

A. He helped to put it in.

Q. About how long were these Indians there before they were arrested?

A. About two weeks.

Q. Who arrested them—Agent Vore?

A. They were arrested by Lieut. Carpenter.

Q. Hadn't they been arrested before by Agent Vore?

A. No, sir.

Q. Didn't they seem to come there as guests of the Omahas?

A. No, sir.

Q. How did they come?

A. They came as Indians, and said they wanted to go back to their old land, or find some place to work, and that if the Omahas would give them some land they would remain with them.

Q. Do these Omahas speak the English language?

A. A very few of them.

Q. None of these Indians here can speak English?

A. No, sir.

Q. About how much cultivated land is there at the Agency?

A. I couldn't tell.

Q. Do you have any idea of the amount?

A. I suppose they have in about 1,500 acres of wheat.

Q. How many Omaha Indians are there?

A. 1083, I believe, at the last count.

Q. That would be about an acre and a half to the Indian?

A. Of wheat ground—yes, sir. They have corn ground as much as that, or more, too.

Q. That would make about three acres to the Indian?

A. Yes, sir.

Q. Do they cultivate this land?

A. Yes, sir.

Q. How do the Omahas live?

A. They live very well.

Q. Does the government furnish them anything?

A. Nothing but farm implements.

Q. The government has an agent there?

A. Yes, sir.

Q. Is there not from time to time annuities paid them by the government?

A. There has been none paid for going on three years now.

Q. Does the government furnish them any clothes?

A. No, sir, all the annuities they have is in money.

Q. Have these Indians received any better clothes since they came to Fort Omaha, or are the clothes they have on now the same they had when arrested?

A. Some they had, and some were given them.

Q. Who furnished them?

A. I don't know. Several persons who came there gave them things.

Q. They didn't have as good clothes as these when they came to Omaha Agency, did they?

A. No, sir, hardly so good.

Q. Are all the Indians at the barracks dressed as well as these?

A. No, sir.

Q. These are the better dressed ones and the better look-ing ones?

A. Yes, sir; for that matter they all look alike.

RE-DIRECT EXAMINATION BY MR. WEBSTER

Q. During the stay of these Poncas at the Agency, were they receiving any annuities from the government?

A. No, sir, not that I know of. At one time, a day or two before they were taken away by Lieut. Carpenter, they received some rations from the agent at the Omaha Agency.

Q. State what objections the Omahas had, if any, to the Poncas remaining upon these lands at the Omaha reservation?

A. They had no objection at all. I know from what the Omahas told me.

[Objected to by counsel for the government, as incom-petent and immaterial. Overruled.]

Mr. Webster—You may state the facts.

A. They said they wanted the Poncas to come back there and live with them; they had more land than they needed, and they could sell them part of their land and they could join together and live as one tribe of Indians. They were willing to have them come and take part of their land, and try to become citizens, as they were trying.

The Court—Were the Poncas ever any part of the Omaha tribe?

Mr. Webster—No, sir, they have simply inter-married to some extent.

RE-CROSS-EXAMINATION BY MR. LAMBERTSON

Q. State whether these Indians submitted themselves

to the authority of the Omaha Indians, or the Omaha chiefs? Were they governed in the same manner the Omahas were, and followed the same pursuits?

A. Yes, sir.

Q. And obeyed the Omaha chiefs?

A. They took advice, of course, of the Omaha chiefs.

Q. Were they governed by the same form as the Omaha Indians?

A. Yes, sir.

Q. They submitted themselves to the same rules, customs and habits as the Omahas?

A. Yes, sir.

Mr. Webster—Do the Omahas have any chiefs?

A. They have no chiefs now.

Q. Then there was no part of the Omahas commanding these Poncas?

A. No, sir.

Q. About all there was about that was that they simply advised together, and consulted as to what was best to be done?

A. Yes, sir.

Mr. Lambertson—Is there any head man in the Omaha tribe?

A. No, sir, not now. There was some time ago, last summer—but they put away all their chiefs and head men.

Mr. Webster—They live like white men, then?

A. They try to.

LIEUT. WILLIAM L. CARPENTER

Sworn on behalf of the relators, and examined in chief by Mr. Webster, testified as follows:

Q. Do you have immediate charge of these Indians?

A. I have.

Q. State whether you are the officer who made the arrest at the Omaha Agency?

A. I am.

Q. Will you state the date of that arrest?

A. It was on Sunday, in the latter part of March, the last week in March. I would have to look at a calendar.

Q. State whether prior to that time you had been acquainted personally with these Poncas?

A. I had never seen them at all before.

Q. At the time they were arrested by you, state in what manner they were dressed—whether they were wearing citizens' clothes or not?

A. The majority of the men were dressed in citizens' clothes. Only two, I think, wore blankets and leggings.

Q. State what you know of these Indians having been engaged in labor and agriculture at the Omaha Agency at the time of, and prior to their arrest.

A. I don't know anything on that subject from my own knowledge—nothing but what I have heard.

Q. Did you, by conversation or otherwise, acquire any knowledge as to what their habits had been at the Omaha Agency?

[Objected to by counsel for the government as incompetent, immaterial and irrelevant. Sustained.]

Mr. Webster—After you had brought these Indians to Fort Omaha, you may state what kind of dress they continued to wear from the day of their arrest by you, up to the present time?

A. Some of them wore the same clothing they are wearing now.

Q. State what these Indians have been doing while under your charge, as to laboring, and their desire to labor.

A. About ten days ago two of the Indians stated they were willing to work. They had been sick for some time.

[Objected to as immaterial by counsel for the government. Sustained.]

Mr. Webster—State from your observation of these Indians, and the labor which they have performed, what skill and knowledge they have as laborers?

[Objected to and sustained.]

CROSS-EXAMINED MR. LAMBERTSON

Q. How many chiefs are there.

[Objected to by counsel for relators as improper cross-examination. Sustained.]

Mr. Lambertson—State the names of the parties arrested?

[Objected to by counsel for the relators as immaterial, and on the ground that the returns show that.]

The Court—Why is that material?

Mr. Lambertson—To show that these Indians have their chiefs, to whom they profess allegiance.

The Court—You will have to make the witness your own to do that.

STANDING BEAR,

One of the relators, sworn on the part of the relators, and examined in chief by Mr. Webster, through the witness Hamilton, who was sworn as interpreter, testified as follows:

Mr. Lambertson—Does this court think an Indian is a competent witness?

The Court—They are competent for every purpose in both civil and criminal courts. The law makes no distinction on account of race, color, or previous condition.

Mr. Webster (to the interpreter)—Ask him to state when it was they left their reservation to go to the Indian Territory?

A. He says it is about two years since they left.

Q. Ask him to state the manner in which they lived on their old reservation, what labor they performed, and what success they had?

A. He says, we lived well; I had my land, and raised enough so I could get along nicely. My children were going to school, we had a good school, and everything going nicely.

Q. Ask him whether his people were working when they lived up there?

A. He says they were all working hard.

Q. Ask him what they were doing up there to become like white men?

The Court—What sort of white men? You had better limit that a little.

Mr. Webster—Well, civilized.

A. He says the white men are great workers, some of them, and some are not. He says it is about the same way with the Indians—some want to work, and some don't. He says he wants to work, and become like a white man, and that he has tried his best.

Q. Ask him when they left their reservation where they went to first, whether to the Omaha reservation?

A. He says no, they didn't go there; they went south to the Indian Territory.

Q. Ask him how they came to go down there. Have him tell the story as to how they came to go down there?

[Objected to by counsel for government on the ground the inquiry here is solely as to whether these Poncas have dissolved their tribal relations. The question was withdrawn.]

Mr. Webster—Ask him how he and his people lived in the Indian Territory after they got down there, what they had, whether they worked, and what kind of clothes they wore? Ask him further, what they did still after they arrived there to become like civilized white men, and then let him tell the story.

Mr. Lambertson—I want questions put to him, and let him answer the questions.

A. He says, when I got down there, I saw the land, and the land was not good to my eye; some places it looked good, but you kick up the soil a little, and you found lots of stones. It was not fit to farm. When we got down there we heard we were going to get clothing, and get money, and everything that we wanted, but I have not seen it yet. When I was told to go down there, I thought, perhaps, the land was good, and I could make a living, but when I got down there it was entirely different from the land in my own home. I couldn't plow, I couldn't sow any wheat, and we all got sick, and couldn't do anything. It seemed as though I had no strength in my body at all. The hot climate didn't agree with me. But when I came back here I seemed to get strength every day. Instead of our tribe becoming prosperous, they died off every day during the time. From the time I went down there until I left, one hundred and fifty-eight of us died. I thought to myself, God wants me to live, and I think if I come back to my old reservation he will let me live. I got back as far as the Omahas, and they brought me down here. I see you all here to-day. What have I done? I am brought here, but what have I done? I don't know.

It seems as though I haven't a place in the world, no place to go, and no home to go to, but when I see your faces here, I think some of you are trying to help me, so that I can get a place sometime to live in, and when it comes my time to die, to die peacefully and happy. (This was spoken in a loud voice, and with much emphasis.)

The Court—Tell the witness to keep cool.

Mr. Webster—Have him state what they did by way of farming and labor while they were down in the Indian Territory.

A. He says they couldn't farm, all the work they did was to haul wood sometimes to the agent, and work around the Agency, what work they could do.

Q. Ask him if they were all ready and willing to work if they had had any work to do?

A. He says yes, if there had been any work to do. They would have all worked if there had been any farming; they all farmed on their own reservation, they all had farms, and all had work to do. Down there, there was no land to farm, and they all got sick, and were not able to work.

Q. Ask him if they had any schools down there, or anything by way of educating the children?

A. He says they had no schools there.

Q. Ask him how many there were in his band of Poncas at the time he left the Indian Territory?

A. He says about fifty.

Q. Ask him how many came away with him when he came to the Omaha reservation?

A. He says thirty.

Q. Ask him whether the others are still in the Indian Territory?

A. He says he thinks some may be on the road back. He heard some were on the road up here.

Q. Ask him how many chiefs of the tribe are down there with the others in the Indian Territory?

A. He says seven.

Q. Ask him why he and the others left the tribe in Indian Territory and came to the Omaha reservation?

A. He says it was hard for him to stay there, and he thought perhaps if he could come up here he could save his wife and child, the only child he has living, and that is why he came up—to save them, and to get a living for them some place else, if he could.

Q. Ask him how many of his children died in the Indian Territory before he came away?

A. He says two died down there. He says his son could talk English and write, and was a great help to him when he was on White Creek, and whenever he thinks of it, it makes him feel very bad.

Q. Ask him what he and those who came with him meant to do when they came north—how they meant to earn a living?

[Objected to by counsel for the government as immaterial. Overruled.]

A. He says he thought it was necessary to earn a living by work, and that is what he wanted to do, and that he thought if he came north he could get his land back and go to work and earn his living in that way.

Q. Ask him when they left the tribe whether they intended to stay away from the tribe?

A. He says when he left, they asked if he was ever coming back, and he told them if he ever came back it would not be to stay; that he wanted to go to a place where they could all work and earn their own living.

Q. Ask him what he intended to do by way of becoming like civilized white men?

A. He says in his travels he has seen a great many white people, and he finds them all working wherever he goes—farming, building houses, and that they have cattle and everything they want; all they want to eat, and he thinks if he has a chance he can do just the same, and that is the way he thought he would do.

The Court—That is the reason he left?

A. Yes, sir.

Mr. Webster—Ask him whether the others that came away with him intended to do what he did?

[Objected to by counsel for the government as incompetent.]

The Court—He may state if he knows.

A. He says they all wanted to do the same—to work and earn a living.

Q. Ask him, if he was released from his imprisonment, whether he intends to go back to the tribe, or what he intends to do?

[Objected to by counsel for the government. Question withdrawn.]

Q. Ask him whether they all intended to put in crops on these lands of the Omahas?

A. He says that was the intention of all.

Q. Ask him whether, after the time they left the Indian Territory, he intended to continue to exercise his powers as chief, or whether they simply acted together as friends?

[Objected to by counsel for the government as leading. Overruled.]

A. He says he didn't consider himself a chief; he didn't

consider himself as their head man, but looked upon himself and the rest as being alike.

Q. Ask him whether, when they advised with him, it was simply in a social way, because of his having been a chief, or whether they recognized any authority in him.

A. He says he felt himself to be as poor as the rest of them.

Q. That is after they left the tribe?

A. Yes, sir.

Q. Ask him to state whether he sent his own children to school?

[Objected to as immaterial. Sustained.]

CROSS-EXAMINATION BY MR. LAMBERTSON

Q. Ask him what was the number of people in the band of which he was chief in the Indian Territory.

A. He says about fifty.

Q. Ask him how many of his particular band he left in the Indian Territory?

A. He says only three of his band he brought with him. The rest of his band are there yet. He brought Yellow-Horse, Long-Runner, and Chicken Hunter, these men and their families.

Q. About how many families of his band did he leave in the Indian Territory!

A. He says about forty people.

Q. Ask him how many families?

A. He says about thirty families; there are about twenty that are married. There are few children; the children are dead.

Q. Ask him if any members of any other band except his own came with him?

A. He says there was.

Q. Ask him how many?

A. He says there was one chief of some other band. He says this other chief had six men with him. Of course he has his family and some of his band.

Q. Ask him how many compose his band, when he is in the Indian Territory?

A. He says about fifty-six. That was his band when he went to the Indian Territory.

Q. And there were fifty when he left?

A. Yes, sir.

Q. Ask him how many of the band of which he was chief died during the time he was in the Indian Territory?

[Objected to as immaterial.]

Mr. Lambertson—Ask him how many of his own band came with him, that is including his own family. Assuming that he had fifty in his band in the Indian Territory, how many of that fifty came with him?

A. He says, taking the men, women, and children that came with him, there were twenty. He says, counting his family, and all that came with him out of his band.

Q. Ask him if he was chief or head man over these Indians now here and those in the Indian Territory?

A. He says, I was not the head man; I don't consider myself any better than they are.

Q. Was that after he got out of the Indian Territory?

A. Yes, sir; after we left the Indian Territory.

Q. Ask him who came with him from the reservation in Dakota to the Indian Territory.

[Objected to as improper cross-examination by counsel for the relators. Sustained.]

Mr. Lambertson—Ask him when he went to the Indian Territory the first time?

A. He says the time he went down there was the year before they planted corn, it was the year before they were taken down the second time.

Q. Ask him if he remained there until the other Indians came down?

[Objected to by counsel for the relators as improper cross-examination. Overruled.]

A. He says no, he did not stay there. He says he was left down there without an interpreter, to make his way back the best he could, because he would not pick out a piece of land there that he liked.

Q. How long was he left there before the other Indians came down?

A. He says it was in the spring they were taken down from their reservation. He says he would like to tell the whole thing over from the time he was taken down first until they were all taken down.

Mr. Lambertson (to Mr. Webster)—Are you willing he should?

Mr. Webster—No.

Mr. Lambertson (to the witness)—Ask him if while they were in the Indian Territory the government provided them with wagons and farming implements?

[Objected to by counsel for the relators as improper cross-examination and as immaterial. Overruled.]

A. He says they got some wagons and some mowing machines.

Q. Ask him if they took their wagons with them when they left the Agency in the Indian Territory?

A. He says they came in wagons.

Q. Ask him if the wagons which they came in from the Indian Territory to the Omaha Agency were the same wagons that were furnished by the government?

A. He says two of the wagons they have were given to them on their former reservation, and the other is one he bought himself—a light spring wagon.

Mr. Webster—Does he mean the Ponca reservation?

A. Yes, sir, up above.

Mr. Lambertson—Ask him if when he left the Indian Territory the other members of the tribe were willing to remain?

[Objected to by counsel for the relators as immaterial and irrelevant. Sustained.]

Mr. Lambertson—Ask him if, when he left the Indian Territory, he informed the agent that he was going away to live for himself and take care of himself?

A. He says he told the agent several times he wanted to go, and asked him to help us get away to our own lands. He says he told him he was coming away to try and save the rest of his family and find some place where he could work and make a living.

Q. Ask him when he left the Indian Territory, whether he intended to go back to their former reservation in Dakota Territory, or did they intend to go to the Omaha reservation?

A. He says he wanted to go on his own land, that had always been his own land; that he never sold it, and that is where he wanted to go to; that his son when he died made him promise if ever he went back there that he would take his bones there and bury him, and that he has got his bones in a box, and that if ever he goes there he will bury his bones there; that there is where he wants to live the rest of his life, and that there is where he wants to be buried.

Q. Ask him if he wants to live in the same manner in which he lived when in the Dakota reservation?

A. He says he might go there and work until he was blind, but that would not change his color; that he would be an Indian in color, but he wants to go and work and become a citizen.

Q. Ask him if he wants to live as the Omaha Indians live on the Omaha reservation?

[Objected to by counsel for the relators as being too indefinite. Sustained.]

Mr. Lambertson—What I desire to ask him is, at the time he came away, if he intended to continue in the same pursuits as when he was arrested, to adopt the same habits and customs as the Omaha Indians.

[Objected to same as before.]

The Court—He may answer.

A. He says that before he was brought down here he didn't know hardly what to do—whether to remain with the Omahas, or to go up to his old reservation; that the Omahas wanted him to stay there. They said they had better all stay there and farm this summer, and then go up this fall; that if they went up there now they would have a hard time to get along, and if they staid there this summer they would help them so they could have a good start after they got to their old reservation.

Q. Ask him whether during the time he was at the Omaha reservation the government issued him and his band rations or provisions?

A. He says the agent issued rations to his band once. He don't know whether they were issued from the government or were bought. It was issued only once. (The interpreter adds that he was the person who weighed out the rations the time referred to.)

With this the testimony closed, the relators resting their case at this point, and no testimony whatever being introduced on behalf of the government.

CHAPTER IX

What the Attorneys Had to Say to the Court

At the conclusion of the testimony of Standing Bear, the government having no evidence to offer, the argument for the Indians was opened by Hon. J. L. Webster. He first enquired, after a brief recital of the wrongs and cruelties which had so long been practised upon the Indians, how the government of the United States got titles to land, and said titles come in three ways—first by discovery; second by conquest; third by purchase.

He maintained that the government could not claim title to this land by discovery. The landing of white men upon the eastern shore of this continent could not give a title to the little piece of land on which the Poncas then resided at the mouth of the Niobrara river. A title by discovery did not give a fee simple to the soil, if it was occupied, but only political control.

The government of the United States could never acquire a title by conquest, for it had never been at war with the Ponca tribe. These two peoples had always been on the most friendly terms. The government had never purchased the land, and, therefore, the title to it still remained in the Poncas. Mr. Webster then discussed the questions relating to Indian tribes as separate nations, the effect of the fourteenth amendment to the Constitution,

91

citizenship of Indians, the use of the army in their control, and made a thorough and able review of the whole problem, claiming that there was no law for the removal of the Poncas to the Indian Territory, or for keeping them there by force, or for returning those who had escaped, and asked the absolute discharge of Standing Bear and his party.

Mr. Webster, who occupied about six hours in the delivery of his argument, was followed by the Government Attorney, Hon. G. M. Lambertson, who opened his argument with a very high commendation of the course of Messrs. Poppleton and Webster in volunteering their services, without the hope of reward, in defence of those helpless Indians. He claimed that Standing Bear was not entitled to the protection of the writ of *habeas corpus*, not being a person or citizen under the law. His argument occupied about five hours, and was very ingenious and eloquent.

Hon. A. J. Poppleton followed in a very powerful argument. He traced the history of the writ of *habeas corpus* from its origin, and claimed that it applied to every *human being*. He appealed on the behalf of these Indians as *men*, and showed that the position taken by the government counsel undermined the very foundations of human liberty. His argument consumed about four hours.*

*[The *Omaha Daily Herald* for May 3, 4, 6, and 7 presents Webster's and Poppleton's arguments in some detail. Lambertson's speech is dismissed much as above, with the additional observation that his argument was based principally on Chief Justice Roger B. Taney's decision in the Dred Scott case—no doubt a reference to the finding in the famous 1857 case that Negroes did not possess rights of citizenship entitling them to sue in federal courts. It is possible to reconstruct, from Poppleton's rebuttal and Dundy's opinion, other major points of Lambert-

Judge Dundy then allowed Standing Bear to address the court on his own behalf. The court room was at this time filled with leading citizens of the State, prominent officers of the army and their wives. Standing Bear's speech made a profound impression on all who heard it. He claimed that, although his skin was of a different hue, yet he was a man, and that God made him. He said he was not a savage, and related how he had saved the life of a soldier whom he had found on the plains, starved, and almost frozen to death, and of a man who had lost his way on the trackless prairie, whom he had fed and guided to his destination. In spite of the orders of the court and the efforts of the bailiffs, he was greeted with continual rounds of applause. At the conclusion of his speech, court adjourned, and the judge took several days to consider the matter.

---

son's argument: he attempted to draw a parallel with early English usage restricting the writ of habeas corpus to certain classes of persons, and he noted the lack of a legal precedent or provision allowing suit by Indians. He apparently asserted that an 1871 statute forbidding further treaty making with Indian tribes released the government from its obligation to obtain the Poncas' consent for their removal (an argument Poppleton countered by citing the specification in the law that it was not to be construed as abrogating existing treaties). Raising a very live issue in the national controversy over Indian policy, he expatiated on Indian atrocities, probably arguing that Indians were unfit to hold the legal rights of a civilized nation. Webster had preempted the defense's possible recourse to an 1870 report of the Senate Judiciary Committee which concluded that the Fourteenth Amendment had no effect on Indian tribes by pointing to its exemption of those Indians who had dissolved their tribal relations. Thus Standing Bear's relationship to his tribe was an important point in the case. —*ed. note*]

CHAPTER X

Standing Bear Released — Decision of Judge Elmer S. Dundy

United States ex rel. Standing Bear, vs. George Crook, a Brigadier-General of the Army of the U.S. Before Elmer S. Dundy, U.S. District Judge for Nebraska. *Habeas corpus.**

An Indian is a *person* within the meaning of the *habeas corpus* act, and as such is entitled to sue out a writ of *habeas corpus* in the federal courts, when it is shown that the petitioner is deprived of liberty under color of authority of the United States, or is in custody of an officer in violation of the constitution, or a law of the United States, or in violation of a treaty made in pursuance thereof.

The right of expatriation is a natural, inherent, and inalienable right, and extends to the Indian as well as to the more fortunate white race.

The Commissioner of Indian Affairs has ample authority for removing from an Indian reservation all persons found thereon without authority of law, or whose presence may be detrimental to the peace and welfare of the Indians.

The military power of the government may be employed to effect such removal. But when the removal is effected, it is the duty of the troops to convey the persons so removed by the most convenient and safe route, to the civil authorities of the judicial district in which the offence may be committed, to be proceeded against in due course of law.

*[Dundy's opinion was filed on May 12.—*ed. note*]

In time of peace no authority, civil or military, exists for transporting Indians from one section of the country to another, without the consent of the Indians, nor to confine them to any particular reservation against their will, and where officers of the government attempt to do this, and arrest and hold Indians who are at peace with the government, for the purpose of removing them to, and confining them on, a reservation in the Indian Territory, they will be released on *habeas corpus.*

A. J. POPPLETON and
JNO. L. WEBSTER,
For the Relators.
G. M. LAMBERTSON, *U.S. Att'y.*
For the Government.

The facts are fully stated in the opinion of the court.

DUNDY, JUDGE

During the fifteen years in which I have been engaged in administering the laws of my country, I have never been called upon to hear or decide a case that appealed so strongly to my sympathy as the one now under consideration. On the one side we have a few of the remnants of a once numerous and powerful, but now weak, insignificant, unlettered and generally despised race. On the other, we have the representative of one of the most powerful, most enlightened, and most christianized nations of modern times. On the one side we have the representatives of this wasted race coming into this national tribunal of ours asking for justice and liberty to enable them to adopt our boasted civilization and to pursue the arts of peace, which have made us great and happy as a nation. On the other side we have this magnificent, if not magnanimous, government, resisting this application with the determination of sending these people back to the country which is to them less desirable than perpetual imprisonment in their own native land. But I think it is creditable to the heart and mind of the brave and distinguished officer who is made respondent herein, to say that he has no sort of sympathy in the business in which he is forced by his position to bear a part so conspicuous. And so far as I am individually concerned, I think it not improper to say that if the strongest possible sympathy could give the relators title to freedom, they would have been restored to liberty the moment the arguments in their behalf were closed. No examination of further thought would then have been necessary or expedient. But in a country where liberty is regulated by law, something more satisfactory and enduring than mere sympathy must furnish and constitute the rule and basis of judicial action. It follows that this case must be examined and decided on principles of law, and that unless the relators are entitled to their discharge under the constitution or laws of the United States, or some treaty made in pursuance thereto, they must be remanded to the custody of the officer who caused their arrest, to be returned to the Indian Territory, which they left without the consent of the government.

On the 8th of April, 1879, the relators, Standing Bear and twenty-five others, during the session of the court held at that time at Lincoln, presented their petition, duly verified, praying for the allowance of a writ of *habeas corpus*, and their final discharge from custody thereunder.

The petition alleges in substance that the relators are Indians who have formerly belonged to the Ponca tribe of Indians, now located in the Indian Territory; that they had some time previously withdrawn from the tribe and completely severed their tribal relations therewith, and had adopted the general habits of the whites, and were then endeavoring to maintain themselves by their own exertions, and without aid or assistance from the general government; that whilst they were thus engaged, and without being guilty of violating any of the laws of the United States, they were arrested and restrained of their liberty, by order of the respondent, George Crook.

The writ was issued and served on the respondent on the 8th day of April, and the distance between the place where the writ was made returnable and the place where the relators were confined being more than twenty miles, ten days were allotted in which to make return.

On the 18th of April the writ was returned, and the authority for the arrest and detention is therein shown. The substance of the return to the writ, and the additional statement since filed, is that the relators are individual members of, and connected with the Ponca tribe of Indians; that they had fled or escaped from a reservation situated some place within the limits of the Indian Territory; had departed therefrom without permission from the government, and at the request of the Secretary of the Interior the General of the army had issued an order which required the respondent to arrest and return the relators to their tribe in the Indian Territory, and that pursuant to the said order, he had caused the relators to be arrested on the Omaha Indian reservation, and that they were in his custody for the purpose of being returned to the Indian Territory.

It is claimed upon the one side, and denied upon the other, that the relators had withdrawn, and severed for all time, their connection with the tribe to which they belonged. And upon this point alone was there any testimony produced by either party hereto. The other matters stated in the petition, and the return to the writ, are conceded to be true, so that the questions to be determined are purely questions of law.

On the 8th of March, 1859, a treaty was made by the United States with the Ponca tribe of Indians, by which a certain tract of country north of the Niobrara river, and west of the Missouri was set apart for the permanent home of the said Indians, in which the government agreed to protect them during their good behavior. But just when, or how, or why, or under what circumstances the Indians left their reservation in Dakota and went to the Indian Territory does not appear.

JURISDICTION OF COURT

The district attorney very earnestly questions the jurisdiction of the court to issue the writ and to hear and determine the case made herein, and has supported his theory with an argument of great ingenuity and much ability. But nevertheless, I am of the opinion that his premises were erroneous, and his conclusions therefore wrong and unjust. The great respect I entertain for that officer, and the very able manner in which his views were presented, make it necessary for me to give somewhat at length the reasons which lead me to this conclusion.

The district attorney discussed at length the reasons which led to the origin of the writ of *habeas corpus*, and the character of, and proceedings and practice in connection therewith in the parent country. It was claimed that the laws of the realm limited the right to sue out this writ to the *free subjects* of the kingdom and that none others came within the benefit of such beneficent laws. And reasoning from analogy, it is claimed that none but American citizens are entitled to sue out this high prerogative writ in any of the federal courts. I have not examined the English laws regulating the suing out of the writ, nor have I thought it necessary so to do. Of this I will only observe that if the laws of England are as they are claimed to be, they will appear at a disadvantage when compared with our own. This only proves that the laws of a limited monarchy are sometimes less wise and humane than the laws of our own good republic—that whilst the Parliament of Great Britain was legislating in behalf of the favored few, the Congress of the United States was legislating in behalf of all mankind who come within our jurisdiction.

Section 751 of the "Revised Statutes" declares that "the supreme court and the circuit and district courts shall have power to issue writs of *habeas corpus.*" Section 752 confers the power to issue writs on the judges of said courts within their jurisdiction, and declares this to be "for the purpose of inquiry into the cause of restraint of liberty." Section 753 restricts the power, limits the jurisdiction, and defines the cases where the writ may properly issue. That may be done under this section where the prisoner "is in custody under or by color of authority of the United States,   *   *   *   or is in custody for an act

done or omitted in pursuance of a law of the United States, *
* * or in custody in violation of the constitution or of a law
or treaty of the United States." Thus it will be seen that when a
person is in custody or deprived of his liberty, under color of
authority of the United States, or in violation of the constitution
or laws or treaties of the United States, the federal judges have
jurisdiction, and the writ can properly issue. I take it that the
true construction to be placed upon this act is this: That in *all*
cases where federal officers, civil or military, have the custody
and control of a person, claimed to be unlawfully restrained of
liberty, that they are *then* restrained of liberty under color of
authority of the United States, the federal courts can properly
proceed to determine the question of unlawful restraint because
no other courts can properly do so. In the other instance, the
federal courts and judges can properly issue the writ in *all* cases
where the *person* is alleged to be in custody in violation of the
constitution or a law or treaty of the United States. In such a
case it is wholly immaterial what *officer*, state or federal, has
custody of the person seeking the relief. These relators may be
entitled to the writ in either case. Under the first paragraph they
certainly are, that is, if an Indian can be entitled to it at all,
because they are in custody of a federal officer under color of
authority of the United States, and they may be entitled to the
writ under the other paragraph before recited, for the reason,
as they allege, that they are restrained of liberty in violation of
a provision of their treaty before referred to. Now, it must be
borne in mind that the *habeas corpus* act describes applicants
for the writ as *"persons"* or *"parties,"* who may be entitled thereto. It nowhere describes them as *citizens*, nor is citizenship in
any way or place made a qualification for sueing out the writ,
and in the absence of express provision or necessary implication,
which would require the interpretation contended for by the
district attorney, I should not feel justified in giving the words
person and *party* such a narrow construction. The most natural,
and therefore most reasonable way, is to attach the same mean-

ing to *words* and *phrases* when found in a statute that is attached to them when and where found in general use. If we do so in this instance, then the question cannot be open to serious doubt. Webster describes a person as "a living soul; a self conscious being; a moral agent; especially a living human being; a man, woman or child; an individual of the human race." This is comprehensive enough, it would seem, to include even an Indian. In describing and defining generic terms, the first section of the revised statutes declares that the word *person* includes co-partnerships and corporations. On the whole it seems to me quite evident that the comprehensive language used in this section is intended to apply to all mankind, as well the relators as the more favored white race. This will be doing no violence to language, nor to the spirit or letter of the law, nor to the intention, as it is believed, of the law-making power of the government.

I must hold, then, that *Indians*, and consequently the relators, are *persons*, such as are described by and included within the laws before quoted. It is said, however, that this is the first instance on record in which an Indian has been permitted to sue out and maintain a writ of *habeas corpus* in a federal court, and *therefore*, the court must be without jurisdiction in the premises. This is a *non sequitur*. I confess I do not know of another instance where this has been done, but I can also say that the occasion for it perhaps has never before been so great. It may be that the Indians think it wiser and better in the end to resort to this peaceful process than it would be to undertake the hopeless task of redressing their own alleged wrongs by force of arms. Returning reason, and the sad experience of others similarly situated, has taught them the folly and madness of the arbitrament of the sword. They can readily see that any serious resistance on their part would be the signal for their utter extermination. Have they not then chosen the wiser part, by resorting to the very tribunal erected by those they claim have wronged and oppressed them? This, however, is not the tribunal of their own choice, but it is the *only* one into which they can lawfully go for deliverance. It cannot therefore be fairly said that because no Indian ever before invoked the aid of this writ in a federal court, that the rightful authority to issue it does not exist. Power and authority rightfully conferred does not necessarily cease to exist in consequence of long non-use. Though much time has elapsed, and many generations have passed away since the passage of the original *habeas corpus* act from which I have quoted, it will not do to say that these Indians cannot avail themselves of its beneficent provisions simply because none of their ancestors ever sought relief thereunder.

Every *person* who comes within our jurisdiction, whether he be European, Asiatic, African, or "native to the manor born," must obey the laws of the United States. Every one who violates them incurs the penalty provided thereby. When a *person* is charged, in a proper way, with the commission of crime, we do not inquire upon the trial in what country the accused was born, nor to what sovereign or government allegiance is due, nor to what race he belongs. The questions of guilt and innocence only form the subjects of inquiry. An Indian then, especially off from his reservation, is amenable to the criminal laws of the United States the same as all other persons. They being subject to arrest for the violation of our criminal laws and being *persons* such as the law contemplates and includes in the description of parties who may sue out the writ, it would, indeed, be a sad commentary on the justice and impartiality of our laws, to hold that Indians, though natives of our own country, cannot test the validity of an alleged illegal imprisonment in this manner, as well as a subject of a foreign government who may happen to be sojourning in this country but owing it no sort of allegiance. I cannot doubt that Congress intended to give to *every person* who might be unlawfully restrained of liberty under color of authority of the United States the right to the writ and a discharge thereon. I conclude then, that so far as the issuing of the writ is concerned, it was properly issued, and that the relators are within the jurisdiction conferred by the *habeas corpus* act.

A question of much greater importance remains for consideration, which, when determined, will be decisive of this whole controversy. This relates to the right of the government to arrest and hold the relators for a time for the purpose of being returned to a point in the Indian Territory, from which it is alleged the Indians escaped. I am not vain enough to think that I can do full justice to a question like the one under consideration. But as the matter furnishes so much valuable material for discussion, and so much food for reflection, I shall try to present it as viewed from my own stand-point, without reference to consequences or criticisms which, though not specially invited, will be sure to follow.

A review of the policy of the government adopted in its dealing with the friendly tribe of Poncas, to which the relators at one time belonged, seems not only appropriate, but almost indispensable to a correct understanding of this controversy. The Ponca Indians have been at peace with the government, and have remained the steadfast friends of the whites for many years. They lived peaceably upon the land and in the country they claimed and called their own.

On the 12th of March, 1858, they made a treaty with the United States by which they ceded all claims to lands except the following tract: "Beginning at a point on the Niobrara river and running due north so as to intersect the Ponca river twenty-five miles from its mouth, thence from said point of intersection up and along the Ponca river twenty miles, thence due south to the Niobrara river, and thence down and along said river to the place of beginning, which tract is hereby reserved for the future homes of said Indians." In consideration of this cession the government agreed "to protect the Poncas in the possession of the tract of land reserved for their future homes, and their persons and property thereon, during good behavior on their part." Annuities were to be paid them for thirty years, houses were to be built, and schools were to be established, and other things were to be done by the government in consideration of said cession. (See page 997, 12, Stat. at large.) On the 10th of March, 1865, another treaty was made, and a part of the other reservation was ceded to the government. Other lands, however, were, to some extent, substituted therefor, and "by way of rewarding them for their constant fidelity to the government and citizens thereof, and with a view of returning to the said tribe of Ponca Indians their old burying grounds and corn fields." This treaty also provides for paying $15,080 for spoliations committed on the Indians.

(See page 675, 14 vol., Stat. at large.)

On the 29th day of April, 1868, the government made a treaty with the several bands of Sioux Indians, which treaty was ratified by the Senate on the 16th of the following February, in and by which the reservations set apart for the Poncas under the former treaties were completely absolved. (15 Statutes at large, page 635.) This was done without consultation with, or knowledge or consent on the part of, the Ponca tribe of Indians.

On the 15th of August, 1876, Congress passed the general Indian appropriation bill, and in it we find a provision authorizing the Secretary of the Interior to use $25,000 for the removal of the Poncas to the Indian Territory, and providing them a home therein, with consent of the tribe. (See page 192, 19 vol., Statues at large.)

In the Indian appropriation bill passed by Congress on the 27th day of May, 1878, we find a provision authorizing the Secretary of the Interior to expend the sum of $30,000 for the purpose of removing and locating the Ponca Indians on a new reservation near the Kaw river.

No reference has been made to any other treaties or laws, under which the right to arrest and remove the Indians is claimed to exist.

The Poncas lived upon their reservation in Southern Dakota and cultivated a portion of the same until two or three years ago, when they removed therefrom, but whether by force or otherwise, does not appear. At all events, we find a portion of them, including the relators, located at some point in the Indian

Territory. *There*, the testimony seems to show, is where the
trouble commenced. Standing Bear, the principal witness, states
that out of 710 Indians who went from the reservation in Dakota
to the Indian Territory 158 died within a year or so, and a great
proportion of the others were sick and disabled, caused in a
great measure, no doubt, from change of climate, and to save
himself and the survivors of his wasted family, and the feeble
remnant of his little band of followers, he determined to leave
the Indian Territory and return to his old home, where, to use
his own language, "he might live and die in peace, and be buried
with his fathers." He also states that he informed the agent of
their final purpose to leave, never to return, and that he and
his followers had finally, fully, and forever servered his and their
connection with the Ponca tribe of Indians, and had resolved to
disband as a tribe, or band, of Indians, and to cut loose from the
government, go to work, become self-sustaining, and adopt
the habits and customs of a higher civilization. To accomplish
what would seem to be a desirable and laudable purpose, all
who were able so to do went to work to earn a living. The
Omaha Indians, who speak the same language, and with whom
many of the Poncas have long since continued to intermarry,
gave them employment and ground to cultivate so as to make
them self-sustaining. And it was when at the Omaha reservation,
and when *thus* employed, that they were arrested by order of
the government for the purpose of being taken back to the
Indian Territory. They claim to be unable to see the justice,
or reason, or wisdom, or *necessity* of removing them by force
from their own native plains and blood relations to a far off
country in which they can see little but new made graves opening
for their reception. The land from which they fled in fear has
no attractions for them. The love of home and native land was
strong enough in the minds of these people to induce them to
brave every peril to return and live and die where they had
been reared. The bones of the dead son of Standing Bear were
not to repose in the land they hoped to be leaving forever, but
were carefully preserved and protected, and formed a part of

what was to them a melancholy procession homeward. Such instances of parental affection, and such love of home and native land may be *heathen* in origin, but it seems to me that they are not unlike *christian* in principle.

What is here stated in this connection is mainly for the purpose of showing that the relators did all they could to separate themselves from their tribe, and to sever their tribal relations, for the purpose of becoming self-sustaining, and living without support from the government. This being so, presents the question as to whether or not an Indian can withdraw from his tribe, sever his tribal relation therewith, and terminate his allegiance thereto, for the purpose of making an independent living, and adopting our own civilization.

If Indian tribes are to be regarded and treated as separate but dependent nations, there can be no serious difficulty about the question. If they are not to be regarded and treated as separate, dependent nations, then no allegiance is owing from an individual Indian to his tribe, and he could, therefore, withdraw therefrom at any time. The question of expatriation has engaged the attention of our government from the time of its very foundation. Many heated discussions have been carried on between our own and foreign governments on this great question, until diplomacy has triumphantly secured the right to every person found within our jurisdiction. This right has always been claimed and admitted by our government, and it is now no longer an open question. It can make but little difference then whether we accord to the Indian tribes a national character or not, as in either case I think the individual Indian possesses the clear and God-given right to withdraw from his tribe and forever live away from it, as though it had no further existence. If the right of expatriation was open to doubt in this country down to the year 1868, certainly since that time no sort of question as to the right can now exist. On the 27th of July, of that year, Congress passed an act, now appearing as sec. 1,999 of the revised statutes, which declares that:

"Whereas, the right of expatriation is a natural and inherent right of all people, indisputable to the enjoyment of the rights of life, liberty, and the pursuit of happiness; and, whereas, in the recognition of this principle the government has freely received emigrants from all nations, and invested them with the rights of citizenship.   *   *   *   *   Therefore any declaration, instruction, opinion, order, or decision of any officer of the United States which denies, restricts, impairs, or questions the right of expatriation, is declared inconsistent with the fundamental principles of the republic." This declaration must forever settle the question until it is re-opened by other legislation upon the same subject. This is, however, only re-affirming in the most solemn and authoritative manner a principle well settled and understood in this country for many years past.

In most, if not all, instances in which treaties have been made with the several Indian tribes, where reservations have been set apart for their occupancy, the government has either reserved the right or bound itself to protect the Indians thereon. Many of the treaties expressly prohibit white persons being on the reservations unless especially authorized by the treaties or acts of Congress for the purpose of carrying out treaty stipulations.

Laws passed for the government of the Indian country, and for the purpose of regulating trade and intercourse with the Indian tribes, confer upon certain officers of the government almost unlimited power over the persons who go upon the reservations without lawful authority. Sec. 2,149 of the revised statutes, authorizes and requires the Commissioner of Indian Affairs, with the approval of the Secretary of the Interior, to remove from any "tribal reservation" any person being thereon without authority of law, or whose presence within the limits of the reservation may, in the judgment of the Commissioner, be detrimental to the peace and welfare of the Indians; the authority here conferred upon the Commissioner fully justifies him in causing to be removed from Indian reservations *all* persons thereon in violation of law, or whose presence thereon may be detrimental to the peace and welfare of the Indians upon the reservations. This applies as well to an Indian as to a white person, and manifestly for the same reason, the object of the law being to prevent unwarranted interference between the Indians and the agent representing the government. Whether such an extensive discretionary power is wisely vested in the Commissioner of Indian Affairs or not, need not be questioned. It is enough to know that the power rightfully exists, and where existing, the exercise of the power must be upheld. If, then, the Commissioner has the right to cause the expulsion from the Omaha Indian reservation of all persons thereon who are there in violation of law, or whose ·presence may be detrimental to the peace and welfare of the Indian, then he must of necessity be authorized to use the necessary force to accomplish his purpose. Where, then, is he to look for this necessary force? The military arm of the government is the most natural and most potent force to be used on such occasions, and sec. 2,150 of the revised statutes especially authorizes the use of the army for this service. The army, then, it seems, is the proper force to employ when intruders and trespassers who go upon the reservations are to be ejected therefrom.

The first sub-division of the revised statutes last referred to provides that "the military forces of the United States may be employed in such manner, and under such regulations as the president may direct:

"First—In the apprehension of every person who may be in the Indian country in violation of law, and in conveying him immediately from the Indian country, by the nearest conveyance and safe route, to the civil authority of the Territory or judicial district in which such person shall be found, to be proceeded against in due course of law." * * * This is the authority under which the military can be lawfully employed to remove intruders from an Indian reservation. What may be done by the troops in such cases is here fully and clearly stated, and it is *this* authority, it is believed, under which the respondent acted.

All Indian reservations held under treaty stipulations with the government must be deemed, and taken to be part of the *Indian country*, within the meaning of our laws on that subject. The relators were found upon the Omaha Indian reservation, that being a part of the Indian country, and not being a part of the Omaha tribe of Indians, they were there without lawful authority, and if the Commissioner of Indian Affairs deemed their presence detrimental to the peace and welfare of the Omaha Indians, he had lawful warrant to remove them from the reservation, and to employ the necessary military force to effect this object in safety. General Crook had the rightful authority to remove the relators from the reservation, and must stand justified in removing them therefrom. But when the troops are thus employed they must exercise the authority in the *manner* provided by the section of the law just read. This law makes it the duty of the troops to convey the parties arrested by the nearest convenient and safe route *to the civil authority of the Territory or judicial district in which such person shall be found, to be proceeded against in due course of law*. The *duty* of the military authorities is here very clearly and sharply defined, and no one can be justified in departing therefrom, especially in time of peace. As General Crook had the right to arrest and remove the relators from the Omaha Indian reservation, it follows from what has been stated that the law required him to convey them to this city, and turn them over to the marshal and United States attorney, to be proceeded against in due course of law. Then proceedings could be instituted against them in either the circuit or district court, and if the relators had incurred a penalty under the law, punishment would follow. Otherwise they would be discharged from custody. But this course was not pursued in this case, neither was it intended to observe the laws in that regard, for General Crook's orders, emanating from higher authority, expressly required him to apprehend the relators, and remove them by force to the Indian Territory, from which it is alleged they escaped. But in what General Crook has done in the premises no fault can be imputed to him. He was simply obeying the orders of his superior officers as a good soldier ought to do, but the orders, as we think, lack the necessary authority of law, and are, therefore, not binding on the relators.

I think I have shown pretty clearly the rightful authority vested in the Commissioner of Indian Affairs in cases like the one under consideration — that he may call on the troops to assist in carrying out his lawful orders, and just *how* and for what *purpose* the authority is vested in him to remove trespassers and intruders from the Indian country.

I have searched in vain for the semblance of any authority justifying the Commissioner in attempting to remove by force any Indians, whether belonging to a tribe or not, to any place, or for any other purpose than what has been stated. Certainly, without some specific authority found in an act of Congress, or in a treaty with the Ponca tribe of Indians, he could not lawfully force the relators back to the Indian Territory to remain and die in that country against their will. In the absence of all treaty stipulations or laws of the United States authorizing such removal, I must conclude that no such arbitrary authority exists. It is true, if the relators are to be regarded as a part of the great nation of Ponca Indians, the government might, in time of war, remove them to any place of safety so long as the war should last, but perhaps no longer unless they were charged with the commission of some crime. This is a war power merely, and exists in time of war only. Every nation exercises the right to arrest and detain an alien enemy, during the existence of a war, and all subjects or citizens of the hostile nations are subject to be dealt with under this rule. But it is not claimed that the Ponca tribe of Indians are at war with the United States so that this war power might be used against them. In fact they are amongst the most peaceable and friendly of all the Indian tribes, and have at times received from the government unmistakable and substantial recognition of their long continued friendship for the whites. In time of peace the war power remains in abeyance, and must be subservient to the civil authority of the government until something occurs to justify its exercise. No fact exists, and nothing has occurred, so far as the relators are concerned, to make it necessary or lawful to exercise such an authority over them. If they could be removed to the Indian Territory by force, and kept there in the same way, I can see no good reason why they might not be taken and kept by force in the penitentiary at Lincoln, or Leavenworth, or Jefferson City, or any other place which the commander of the forces might, in his judgment, see proper to designate. I cannot think, and will not believe, that any such arbitrary authority exists in this country, and until the highest judicial tribunal in this land shall otherwise determine, I shall not be convinced that my conclusions are erroneous.

I have not thought it necessary to consider the question of citizenship so ably presented on both sides, and therefore express no opinion thereon.

The reasoning advanced in support of my views, leads me to conclude:

First. That an *Indian* is a PERSON within the meaning of the laws of the United States, and has therefore the right to sue out a writ of *habeas corpus* in a federal court or before a federal judge, in all cases where he may be confined, or in custody under color of authority of the United States, or where he is restrained of liberty in violation of the constitution or laws of the United States.

Second. That General George Crook, the respondent, being the commander of the military department of the Platte, has the custody of the relators under color of authority of the United States, and in violation of the laws thereof.

Third. That no rightful authority exists for removing by force any of the relators to the Indian Territory, as the respondent has been directed to do.

Fourth. That the Indians possess the inherent right of expatriation as well as the more fortunate white race, and have the

inalienable right to *"life, liberty* and the pursuit of happiness,"
so long as they obey the laws and do not trespass on forbidden
ground. And

Fifth. Being restrained of liberty under color of authority of
the United States, and in violation of the laws thereof, the
relators must be discharged from custody, and it is so ordered.

CHAPTER XI

The Order of Release — Standing Bear's Farewell Addresses

A few days after the decision, Gen. Crook received an order from the Secretary of War ordering the discharge of Standing Bear and his companions. The day before he was to leave, the editor went out to bid him good-bye. The old chief said he had something to say that he did not wish anybody to hear. The editor, Standing Bear and the interpreter went out on a little hill to one side. There he spoke as follows:

When I was brought here a prisoner, my heart was broken. I was in despair. I had no friend in all the big world. Then you came. I told you the story of my wrongs. From that time until now you have not ceased to work for me. Sometimes, in the long days while I have been here a prisoner, I have come out here, and stood on this hill and looked towards the city. I thought there is one man there who is writing or speaking for me and my people. I remember the dark day when you first came to speak to me. I know if it had not been for what you have done for me I would now be a prisoner in the Indian Territory, and many of these who are with me here would have been in their graves. It is only the kind treatment they have received from the soldiers, and the medicine which the army doctor has given them, which has saved their lives. I owe all this to you. I can never pay you for it.

I have traveled around a good deal. I have noticed that there are many changes in this world. You have a good house now to live in. A little while ago I had a house and land and stock. Now I have nothing. It may be that some time you may have trouble. You might lose your house. If you ever want a home come to me or my tribe. You shall never want as long as we have anything. All the tribe in the Indian Territory will soon know what you have done. While there is one Ponca alive you will never be without a friend. Mr. Poppleton and Mr. Webster are my friends. You are my brother.

The old chief then led the way to his lodge, and opening a trunk, he took out a war-bonnet, a tomahawk, and a pair of beaded buckskin leggings. He said, "These leggings are for you, the tomahawk for Mr. Webster, and the war-bonnet for Mr. Poppleton. I wish you to take them and tell them I sent them to them."

The editor suggested that he should go down to the city and present them himself, which he consented to do. The following is the account of the presentation, published at the time in the daily papers:

The decision of Judge Dundy, releasing Standing Bear and his band to civilization went into effect on Monday, May 19th, 1879, and they forthwith took their departure for the locality which they have selected on United States territory. On Sunday, the now liberated chief visited the city, and called at the residence of Hon. J. L. Webster, and Hon. A. J. Poppleton, to whose vindication in the courts he owes his enfranchisement, to express his gratitude by word and by deed. Out of the poverty of his worldly possessions he gave such visible token of his appreciation as he could, while out of the wealth of his human soul, and out of the fulness of his manly heart, he uttered sentiments and expressed purposes which distinguish him as a chief among ten thousand, and as a character—dark though his skin may be, "altogether lovely." He first visited the residence of Mr. Webster, and to that gentleman he presented his tomahawk,

bearing his name. After shaking hands with all present, beginning with the ladies, to whom he said he wished first to pay
respect, he said, addressing Gen. Webster:

STANDING BEAR TO WEBSTER

"You and I are here. Our skins are of a different color, but
God made us both. A little while ago, when I was young, I was
wild. I knew nothing of the ways of the white people.

"I see you have nice houses here. I look at these beautiful
rooms; I would like to have a house too, and it may be after a
while that I can get one, but not so nice a house as this. That is
what I want to do.

"For a great many years—a hundred years or more—the
white men have been driving us out. They are shrewd, sharp
and know how to cheat; but since I have been here I have found
them different. They have all treated me kindly. I am very thank-
ful for it.

"Hitherto, when we have been wronged we went to war to
assert our rights and avenge our wrongs. We took the tomahawk. We had no law to punish those who did wrong; so we
took our tomahawks and went to kill. If they had guns and
could kill us first it was the fate of war.

"But you have found a better way. You have gone into the
court for us, and I find that our wrongs can be righted there.
Now *I have no more use for the tomahawk. I want to lay it down
forever.*"

Uttering these words with eloquent impressiveness, the old
chief stooping down, placed the tomahawk on the floor at his
feet—then standing erect he folded his arms with native dignity
and continued:

"I lay it down; I have no more use for it; *I have found a better
way.*"

Stooping again and taking up the weapon he placed it in Mr.
Webster's hands and said:

"I present it to you as a token of my gratitude. I want you to keep it in remembrance of this great victory which you have gained. I have no further use for it; *I can now seek the ways of peace.*"

MR. WEBSTER'S REPLY

"STANDING BEAR, —I rejoice to know that you and those who are with you desire to become civilized, and like the white people of America. We know that for the last hundred years your tribe has always been the friend and protector of the white people. The ways of the whites may seem to you to be difficult, and hard to learn. Our ancestors were born white, while yours were born red; but a thousand years ago, when they inhabited the central and northern portions of Europe, they followed the same manner of life that you have led. We have progressed slowly from that time until we are now as you see us. I think it is the duty of the government and all the people to aid the friendly and peaceful Indians in every way possible to acquire the arts of civilization.

"When the whites landed on these shores, they found here at least four millions of your people, and now you are reduced to 250,000, and we have absorbed nearly all your lands. I think it a duty we owe to humanity and to God to extend to your people the benefit and protection of our laws. What I have done to relieve you from imprisonment and captivity in the Indian Territory—where, if you had returned your whole band would have been exterminated—was from principle, and as a matter of justice. I shall continue to fight your battles as long as it is necessary to give you the protection of the laws, and I rejoice to know that you have come to believe the tomahawk is of no further service to you, and that you have resolved to seek the ways of peace. I accept the weapon from your hands, and shall preserve it through the years to come, in memory of the effort I have made to prevent the extermination of your people. What

I have done has been a labor of pleasure. I hope you and those who are with you will live to become happy and prosperous, and that any habits of wild life which may still cling to you may drop off as the blighted fruit falls from the trees when shaken by the winds, and that ere long I may hear that you are surrounded with all the comforts and blessings of civilized life."

Leaving Mr. Webster's residence, Standing Bear visited Mr. Poppleton's rooms. He informed Mr. Poppleton that he was about to leave for the north, and he thought he would call and bid him good-bye.

STANDING BEAR TO POPPLETON

He said: "I believe I told you in the court room that God made me and that I was a man.

"For many years we have been chased about as a dog chases a wild beast. God sent you to help me. I thank you for what you have done.

"I want to get my land back. That is what I long for all the time. I wish to live there and be buried with my fathers.

"When you were speaking in the court room of course I could not understand, but I could see that you were trying very hard to release me. I think you are doing for me and my people something that never has been done before.

"If I had to pay you for it, I could never get enough to do it. I have here a relic which has come down to my people through a great many generations. I do not know how old it is; it may be two or three hundred years old. I desire to present it to you for what you have done for me."

Mr. Poppleton, accepting the gift, said to Standing Bear that he was more than repaid for what he may have done, in the satisfaction he felt in having rescued him and his people, and secured their rights to them; and his satisfaction would be all the deeper should they succeed in maintaining themselves in their new relations and achieving the arts and the freedom and peace of civilized life.

The keepsake given by the chief to the great attorney is a rare gift, being esteemed the most sacred, as it is the most venerable object in the possession of the tribe. It resembles a wig, and was worn by the head chief at their most weighty councils. Curiosity-hunters have often sought to secure it at any price in money, but he has to one and all said that money could not buy it. Among occasions on which it has been worn was that of the first treaty—in 1817, we believe—made between the Poncas and the government of the United States. Standing Bear, who is himself sixty years of age, informed us that when he was a little boy his father told him that no one in the tribe knew how old it was, and that it had come into their possession in generations long past.

Appendix

Shortly after the *habeas corpus* case was brought in Omaha, to secure the release of Standing Bear and his associates, Bright Eyes, and her father, Iron Eye, head chief for some years of the Omaha tribe, were sent to the Indian Territory to ascertain the condition of the remainder of the Ponca tribe, who were still held as prisoners in that land. While there, Ke-tha-ska (White Eagle), head chief of the tribe, dictated a letter to the people of the United States, which has been pronounced by Rev. Joseph Cook to be, in many passages, as eloquent as the historic speech of Logan.* The letter is very long. The following are the closing paragraphs:

He had related at great length the dealings of the chiefs with the agents of the government who came to remove them from their lands in Dakota, and had come to the point where the last peremptory order for their departure had been given:—

THE STORY OF WHITE EAGLE

We then separated, and calling all the men of our tribe together, I said to them, "My people, we, your chiefs, have worked

*[James, or John, Logan (c. 1725–80) was an Indian leader in the Ohio and Scioto river valleys. A friend of the whites until some of his family were massacred by white settlers in 1774, he instigated retaliatory

hard to save you from this. We have resisted until we are worn out, and now we know not what more we can do. We leave the matter into your hands to decide. If you say that we fight and die on our lands, so be it." There was utter silence. Not a word more was spoken. We all arose and started for our homes, and there we found that in our absence the soldiers had collected all our women and children together, and were standing guard over them. The soldiers got on their horses, went to all the houses, broke open our doors, took our household utensils, put them in their wagons, and, pointing their bayonets at our people, ordered them to move. They took all our plows, mowers, hayforks, grindstones, farming implements of all kinds, and everything too heavy to be taken on a journey, and locked them up in a large house. We never knew what became of them afterwards. Many of these things of which we were robbed we had bought with money earned by the work of our hands. They promised us more when we should get down here, but we have never received anything in place of them.

We left in our own land two hundred and thirty-six houses which we had built with our own hands. We cut the logs, hauled them, and built them ourselves. We have now, in place of them, six little shanties, built for us by the government. These are one story high, with two doors and two windows. They are full of holes and cracks, and let in the wind and rain. We hear that our own houses which we left in Dakota have all been pulled down. To show how much the tribe have been robbed of we will count the household possessions of a single one of our families in Dakota before we came down. Two stoves, one a kitchen stove and the other a parlor stove, with all the accompanying utensils, two bedsteads, two plows and one double plow, one harrow, one spade, two hayforks, one hand-saw, and one large two-handled

---

raids, precipitating the so-called Dunmore's War of that year. The speech in which he refused to participate in peace negotiations with Lord Dunmore, governor of Virginia, is noted for its eloquence.—*ed. note*]

saw, one grindstone, one hay rake, a cupboard and four chairs. We have now no stoves, chairs, or bedsteads. We have nothing but our tents, and their contents, composed mostly of clothing. The tribe owned two reapers, eight mowers, a flour and saw mill. They are gone from us also. We brought with us twenty-five yoke of oxen. They all died when we got here, partly from the effects of the toilsome journey, and partly by disease. We have not one left. We brought with us five hundred horses, and bought at different times after we arrived two hundred more. We have now been here about two years, and during that time we have lost over six hundred, mostly by death; some were stolen by bad men. We have now not one hundred left of the seven hundred. Our horses died either from the effects of poisonous weeds or disease. The tribe numbered seven hundred when we started. Since we have been here over one hundred and fifty of my people have died.

When people lose what they hold dear to them the heart cries all the time. I speak now to you lawyers who have helped Standing Bear, and to those of you who profess to be God's people. We had thought that there were none to take pity on us and none to help us. We thought all the white men hated us, but now we have seen you take pity on Standing Bear when you heard his story. It may be that you knew nothing of our wrongs, and, therefore, did not help us. I thank you in the name of our people for what you have done for us through your kindness to Standing Bear, and I ask of you to go still further in your kindness and help us to regain our land and our rights. You cannot bring our dead back to life, but you can yet save the living. My heart thinks all the time of our dead. I cry day and night for the men, women, and children who have been killed by this land. My eyes were heavy with weeping, but when I heard of your kindness to some of my people I felt as if I might raise my head and open my eyes to see the coming light. I want to save the remainder of my people, and I look to you for help.

They cry for their land, and I want to give them back that of which they were robbed.

When I went to see the President, and told him how we had been wronged, he said that those who did the deed were gone, and it was among the things of the past. I now ask the President once again through this message, which I send to all the white people of this land, to rectify his mistake. When a man desires to do what is right, he does not say to himself, "It does not matter," when he commits a wrong.

his
KHE-THA-SKA, X (White Eagle).
mark.

EVIDENCE FROM OFFICIAL RECORDS

All the statements of fact contained in this book are fully corroborated by the official reports of the Department of the Interior. The following extracts give a condensed history of the whole transaction. It is hardly likely that any will be so bold as to say this evidence is impeachable, whatever they may say of the statements of the Indians themselves.

WHAT KIND OF INDIANS ARE THE PONCAS?

The Poncas are good Indians. In mental endowment, moral character, physical strength and cleanliness of person they are superior to any tribe I have ever met. —[Report of Indian Commissioner, 1878, p. 65.]

THE PONCA TITLE

Article I. The Ponca tribe of Indians hereby cede and relinquish to the United States all that portion of their present reservation as described in the first article of the treaty of March 12, 1858, lying west of the range line between townships numbers thirty-two (32) and thirty-three (33) north, ranges ten (10) and eleven (11) west of the sixth (6) principal meridian, according to the Kansas and Nebraska survey, estimated to contain thirty thousand acres, be the same more or less.

Article II. In consideration of the cession or release of that portion of the reservation above described by the Ponca tribe of Indians to the government of the United States, the government of the United States, by way of rewarding them for their constant fidelity to the government and citizens thereof, and with a view of returning to the said tribe of Ponca Indians their old burying-grounds and corn-fields, hereby *cede* and *relinquish* to the tribe of Ponca Indians the following described fractional townships, to wit: (townships described in treaty). But it is expressly understood and agreed that the United States shall not be called upon to satisfy or pay the claims of any settlers for improvements upon the lands above ceded by the United States to the Poncas, but the Ponca tribe of Indians shall, out of their own funds, and at their own expense, satisfy said claimants, should any be found upon said lands above ceded by the United States to the Ponca tribe of Indians.—[United States Statutes at large, vol. xiv, page 675.]

HOW THE PONCAS WERE REMOVED

Steps are being taken for the removal of the Poncas from their present location in Southeastern Dakota to the Indian Territory. For this removal, conditioned on the consent of the Poncas, Congress at its last session appropriated $25,000.— [Report of Indian Commissioner, 1876, pp. 16, 17.]

DID THE PONCAS CONSENT?

The title of the old Ponca reservation in Dakota still remains in the Poncas, they having signed no papers relinquishing their title, nor having violated any of the provisions of the treaty by which it was ceded to them by the government. These Indians claim that the government had no right to remove them from their reservation without first obtaining from them by treaty or purchase the title which they have acquired from the government, and for which they had rendered a valuable consideration.—[Report of Indian Commissioner, 1877, p. 101.]

More than three-fourths of the tribe refused to leave their old reservation in Dakota, stating, as reported to me, that they preferred to remain and die on their native heath in defence of their homes, and what they claimed to be their rights in the land composing the reservation on which they were living, than to leave there and die by disease in the unhealthy miasmatic country which they claimed had been selected for them in the Indian Territory.—[Report of Indian Commissioner, 1877, p. 96.]

FATE OF NORTHERN INDIANS SENT TO INDIAN TERRITORY

The effect of a radical change of climate is disastrous, as this (the Pawnee) tribe alone, in the first two years, lost by death over 800 out of its number of 2,376. The northern Cheyennes have suffered severely, and the Poncas, . . . who arrived there in July last, have already lost 36 by death, which, by an ordinary computation, would be the death rate for the entire tribe for a period of four years. In this connection, I recommend the removal of all the Indians in Colorado and Arizona to the Indian Territory.—[E. A. Hayt, in Indian Commissioner's Report, 1877, pp. 5, 6.]

WERE THE PONCAS WRONGED?

In this removal, I am sorry to be compelled to say, the Poncas were wronged. They gave up lands, houses, and agricultural implements. But the removal inflicted a far greater injury upon the Poncas, for which no reparation can be made—the loss by death of many of their number by change of climate.—[Report of Indian Commissioner, 1878, pp. xxxvi and xxxvii.]

WHY IT WAS POSSIBLE TO COMMIT THIS WRONG

My predecessors have frequently called attention to the start-
ling fact that we have within our midst 275,000 people for whom
we provide no law.—[Report of Indian Commissioner, 1876,
p. 9.]

THE COMMISSIONER'S CLAIMS TO ABSOLUTE POWER
OVER INDIANS REGARDLESS OF COURTS

The Commissioner of Indian Affairs says with reference to
the *habeas corpus* case at Omaha, where a writ was served on
General Crook, commanding him to show cause why he holds
Standing Bear and other Ponca Indians as prisoners, that the
United States district-attorney has been directed to appear for
the United States and endeavor to have the writ dismissed. He
takes the ground that under the law, and according to repeated
decisions of the Supreme Court, the Indians stand as wards of
the government, and are under the same relations to the government as minors to their parents or guardians; that the law
forbids them to make contracts, and such contracts if made by
them are void. No attorney has the right or can appear for an
Indian, until authorized to do so by the Indian Department.—
[Associated Press telegram, April 10, 1879.]

Indian Characteristics

The Indians have been so long and so constantly misrepresented by those whose interest it has been to rob them, and have had special facilities for disseminating falsehoods concerning them, that it seems only appropriate to close this little volume with some general statements which are known to be true by all those acquainted with them.

In the first place there never was such a thing as a nomadic tribe of American Indians. The Indian is more strongly attached to the spot where is located his village and graveyard than any other human being. They have fought almost to utter extermination, time and again, in the hope of retaining their lands.

The idea that an Indian is naturally bloodthirsty and delights only in torture and cruelty, is almost too absurd to deserve contradiction. When at peace there are no more generous, kindly and sympathizing people on the earth. It is, however, a fact that when they go to war, they seek to exterminate their enemies, and in the rage of battle seldom spare age or sex.

It is also a fact, which no person desiring the truth to be known will question, that for the last fifteen or twenty years, in nearly every prominent council which has been held with the western Indians, they have earnestly petitioned for schools and farming implements, and many speeches are on record in the government reports protesting against the issue of rations.

Their leading and most intelligent chiefs have said time and again, that as long as rations and clothing were issued to a people they would not work, and they desired the rations stopped, and farming implements issued and schools established in their stead. Any one can arrive at a just conception of the Indian who will take for his first premise, that an Indian is a human being, subject to like passions, desires and ambitions, and adopting the same mode of reasoning, as the other portions of the human race would under similar circumstances.

The prominent traits of Indian character are honesty, generosity, gratitude, attachment to home and country, and love of family and friends. In speaking of one of their traits of character, Gen. George Crook, Commander of the Department of the Platte, says, "The Indian in his nature is in one respect the opposite of the Chinaman. The latter is frugal, even to abstemiousness, and economical to the verge of parsimoniousness; the former frequently at feasts and dances gives away the bulk of his possessions to needy friends and relatives."*

The cause of all our troubles with them may be summed up in the words of the closing paragraph of the above letter. These words should command the attention of the American people. Gen. Crook has been among the Indians for nearly thirty years. He has by force of character and honesty of purpose in all his transactions risen from the

*See letter in *New York Tribune*, Oct. 16th, 1879.

rank of Brevet Second Lieutenant to that of Brigadier-General in the Army of the United States. There is no man in America so well qualified to speak upon the subject, and he says of the Indian:

"When his horses and cattle are big enough to be of service, they are driven off in herds by white renegades; when his wheat and corn and vegetables are almost ready for the market, his reservation is changed, and sometimes, as in the case of the Poncas, he is compelled to abandon everything. Were we to treat some of our foreign immigrants in such a manner, it would not take long to turn them into prowling vagabonds, living by robbery and assassination."

Therefore the solution of the Indian problem lies in these propositions: Acknowledge their manhood and humanity, give them titles in fee simple to their lands, non-transferrable for say twenty years, that their children may become accustomed to their new life; stop the issue of rations, issue to them farming implements, live stock and seeds; extend over them the common school system; protect them from wrong by the regular processes of law; punish the individuals among them who commit crime, after fair trials in the courts, and not hold the tribe responsible, make war and kill innocent persons for the crimes of others; abolish the traderships; let them sell their products where they can get the best prices, and buy where they can buy the cheapest. Then, being equal before the law, and their lives and property protected by it, they will rapidly advance, and the Indian Bureau can close its accounts.

Epilogue

Standing Bear's victory in court was only the opening volley in a reinvigorated battle for reform of Indian policy. In his memoirs Tibbles tells how he decided to join the national crusade. After long talks with Webster and General Crook he resigned his position on the *Omaha Daily Herald* to embark on a fund-raising tour.[1] Concerned about the Poncas still in Indian Territory and fearing that revenge would be taken on the Omahas for befriending Standing Bear, Tibbles and the Omaha Committee—the group of local ministers and other humanitarians who had sent Joseph La Flesche (Iron Eye) and his daughter Susette (Bright Eyes) on the fact-finding trip described in the Appendix—proposed to bring additional suits to test the legal rights of Indians. Moreover, Lambertson had taken steps to appeal Dundy's decision, and the Omaha organization hoped to carry the case to the Supreme Court.

Armed with news clippings on the Ponca story and endorsements from General Crook, the mayor of Omaha, and leading Nebraska clergyman, Tibbles set off in June on a speaking tour of the East. He received an especially

1. Thomas Henry Tibbles, *Buckskin and Blanket Days* (New York, 1957; reprinted Lincoln: University of Nebraska Press, 1969), p. 204.

warm welcome in that center of humanitarian activity, Boston, where philanthropists and friends of the Indian— men like Wendell Phillips, Unitarian minister and reformer Edward Everett Hale, publisher Henry O. Houghton, Mayor Frederick O. Prince, and Henry Wadsworth Long- fellow—established a committee to support the Poncas' cause. After enlisting Bright Eyes and Standing Bear him- self in the "terrible fight with the Indian Ring," Tibbles returned on an extended visit in the fall. By his account, the party took Boston by storm. Bright Eyes, an attractive twenty-five-year-old woman who had been educated in the East and returned to work as a teacher among the Omahas, attracted particular attention: upon meeting her, Longfellow reportedly exclaimed, "*This* is Minnehaha."[2]

Reformist activity picked up sharply after the shooting, at the Ponca agency, of Standing Bear's brother—an acci- dent according to Indian Bureau officials but vengeful wanton murder in the eyes of the humanitarians—and Secretary Schurz was soon cast as an archvillain. Not only did he refuse to return the Poncas to their old home, although he admitted that the tribe had been grievously wronged; he halted appeal proceedings, depriving the humanitarians of an opportunity to obtain a definitive Supreme Court judgment on Indian citizenship. He blamed the Poncas' unfortunate situation on the previous ad- ministration—overlooking that the actual removal had taken place during his own—but felt that moving them back to Dakota would set a bad precedent. He further described the improved condition of the tribe in terms almost as exaggerated as the denunciations issued by his detractors. An exchange in early 1880 with author and

2. Ibid., pp. 210, 218.

reformer Helen Hunt Jackson, who had met Tibbles's group and espoused their cause, gave the secretary an opportunity to air his Indian program. It was thoroughly enlightened for the day and differed little from the proposals of the humanitarians, advocating early allotment of Indian lands in severalty and concomitant granting of citizenship and equal rights before the law. But the reformers were not to be so easily placated: they continued their barrage on Schurz throughout 1880—and indeed until he left office in March, 1881—even though his stand was backed by the Board of Indian Commissioners, the unpaid group of philanthropists who served the Indian Bureau in an advisory capacity.[3]

Meanwhile, Congress got into the act when Senator Henry L. Dawes of Massachusetts, the political liaison of the Boston humanitarians, arranged to have a select committee on which he was serving investigate the Ponca case. Hearings were held throughout the spring of 1880 and Standing Bear and Bright Eyes as well as representatives of the Poncas still on the new reservation appeared as witnesses. E. C. Kemble, the government inspector in charge of the removal, challenged the Indians' story,

3. Helen Hunt Jackson devoted a chapter to the Ponca case in her exposé of federal Indian policy, *A Century of Dishonor* (New York: Harper, 1881). Her correspondence with Schurz is included in the appendix, pp. 359–66.

Fuller considerations of the Ponca controversy in the context of the Indian reform movement may be found in Loring Benson Priest, *Uncle Sam's Stepchildren: The Reformation of United States Indian Policy, 1865–1887* (New Brunswick, N.J.: Rutgers University Press, 1942) pp. 76–80; Stanley Clark, "Ponca Publicity," *Mississippi Valley Historical Review* 29 (March 1943): 495–516; and Robert Winston Mardock, *The Reformers and the American Indian* (Columbia: University of Missouri Press, 1971), pp. 168–91. James T. King focuses on General Crook's role in the affair in "'A Better Way': General George Crook and the Ponca Indians," *Nebraska History* 50 (Fall 1969): 239–56.

contending that they had knowingly agreed to give up their Dakota reservation in exchange for one in Indian Territory and that the eight chiefs who left the inspection party had not been abandoned but had become unhappy and slipped away in the night. Nevertheless, the majority of the committee concluded in their lengthy report of May 31 that they could see "no valid objection . . . to that means of redress which comes nearest to putting these Indians in precisely the condition they were in when E. C. Kemble undertook, without authority of law, to force them from their homes."[4] They recommended passage of a bill then pending which would provide $50,000 for returning the Poncas to their old reservation and restoring their homes, but it encountered opposition and was never reported out of committee.

In the summer the campaign took a new tack as Tibbles and the Omaha reformers devised a more direct approach to aid the Poncas in Indian Territory. In June he visited them—secretly, since unauthorized persons could not legally enter a reservation—and encouraged them to join the small group of their tribesmen who had followed Standing Bear's example and gone back north, where they were being cared for by the Omaha Committee. In an episode that bordered on comic opera, Tibbles was arrested and forcibly ejected from the reservation, although he later pooh-poohed the allegation that he had sneaked into the Ponca camp "disguised as an Indian squaw with a blanket around his shoulders."[5]

Few of the Indians took Tibbles's advice. By this time

4. U.S., Congress, Senate, Select Committee, *Report on Poncas*, 46th Cong., 2d sess., Sen. Rept. 670, p. xix.
5. Tibbles, *Buckskin and Blanket Days*, p. 232.

real progress had been made toward securing adequate housing, farming implements, and school facilities—so much so that in October, 1880, a number of the chiefs and headmen requested permission to visit Washington to arrange the sale of their old reservation and secure a permanent title to the new one. The humanitarians were suspicious of the move—Tibbles accused Schurz of misrepresenting the contents of the memorial and of intimidating the Ponca delegation[6]—but it was apparently motivated by a sincere desire to end the turmoil and settle the matter finally, now that the tribe had become acclimated to Indian Territory.

To ensure as fair a settlement as possible, President Hayes appointed a commission made up of Generals Crook and Nelson A. Miles; William Stickney, a member of the Board of Indian Commissioners; and Walter Allen, one of the Boston committeemen, "to ascertain the facts in regard to [the Poncas'] recent removal and present condition, so far as is necessary to determine the question what justice and humanity require should be done by the government of the United States." In January, 1881, the men interviewed Poncas both from Indian Territory and from Standing Bear's band, who were now living on an island in the Niobrara not included in the Sioux treaty. They found that the removal "was not only most unfortunate for the Indians, resulting in great hardships and serious loss of life and property, but was injudicious and without sufficient cause"; the tribe "had violated no condition of the treaty by which their title to the lands or claim to protection had been forfeited" and thus that claim still existed "in full force and effect." The commission's report,

6. Mardock, *Reformers*, p. 184.

which was heartily endorsed by the president, recommended the allotment of 160 acres to every member of the tribe, either on the old reservation or in Indian Territory; cash compensation for losses; and additional appropriations to provide homes and schools for the Dakota Poncas. In conclusion the commissioners expressed their conviction that "it is of the utmost importance to white and red men alike that all Indians should have the opportunity of appealing to the courts for the protection and vindication of their rights of person and property."[7]

President Hayes forwarded the commission's recommendations to Congress, and they were incorporated in in a bill which was passed on March 31, 1881.[8] But the effects of the Ponca agitation reached even farther: the interest in Indian reform stimulated by the case carried over well into the eighties and culminated in 1887 with the passage of the Dawes allotment act, then seen as the ultimate victory for the humanitarians although in practice it proved disastrous for the tribes. By Tibbles's own evaluation a quarter of a century later, "The outcome had justified us, and we not only had reinstated the Poncas, but we had established the rights of all Indians to turn to the law for protection [and] had weakened the power of a horde of minor but absolute monarchs over a helpless race."[9]

7. Copy of the report in Bourke Diary, January 26, 1881. Bourke's record of the commission's proceedings are included in his diary from December 16, 1880, to January 26, 1881.

8. The provision authorizing those Poncas who so desired to select an allotment on the old Dakota reservation rendered unimportant a decision handed down by Judge Dundy on December 3, 1880. In a suit sponsored by the Omaha Committee and brought by Poppleton and Webster in behalf of the Ponca tribe against Red Cloud and his band of Sioux, Dundy ruled that the Poncas had a legal estate in the reservation and were entitled to possession of it.

9. Tibbles, *Buckskin and Blanket Days*, p. 234.

Tibbles's interest in Indian reform did not end with the resolution of the Ponca dispute, but the tempo of his activity in the movement slackened considerably. In June, 1881, he followed *The Ponca Chiefs* with a second denunciation of governmental policy, a novel entitled *Hidden Power: A Secret History of the Indian Ring*, which he frankly admitted was propaganda. The *Boston Transcript*'s reviewer thought the book "can hardly be praised for literary excellence; yet despite that fact, it cannot help making a strong impression."[10] Tibbles and Bright Eyes were married in the summer of 1881 at the Omaha reservation. Assistant Secretary of the Interior Alonzo Bell acidly noted the event in a letter to former secretary Schurz: ". . . this last act of the pale-face is in the line of other wrongs perpetrated upon this most unfortunate band of Indians. . . . I fear poor Bright Eyes has made a mistake, but I am willing to forgive her if the act has effectually disposed of Tibbles. Even so great a sacrifice may be a rare economy if it gives the Nation a rest from the vexatious borings of the Tibbles school of philanthropy."[11]

The couple continued to lecture intermittently and in 1883 settled down on Bright Eyes's allotment near Bancroft, Nebraska.[12] They farmed there for several years, taking time off in 1886–87 for a speaking tour of England and Scotland. Soon after their return Tibbles began to feel the pull of newspaper life again, and in 1888 he rejoined the editorial staff of the *Omaha World-Herald*. He was on

10. Ibid., p. 235.

11. Alonzo Bell to Carl Schurz, August 15, 1881, in Carl Schurz, *Speeches, Correspondence and Political Papers of Carl Schurz*, ed. by Frederic Bancroft (New York: G. P. Putnam's Sons, 1913), 4: 147–48.

12. The Omahas, fearing that the government might try to move them to Indian Territory as it had the Poncas, petitioned Congress for allotment of their land in severalty. Their request was granted in 1882 and allotments were made the next year.

hand at Pine Ridge as a correspondent during the Ghost Dance difficulties of 1890 and claims to have filed the first press report of the Wounded Knee massacre.[13] It was the last major outrage against the Indian to absorb his attention; the "Indian question" seemed well on its way to being solved.

Thereafter Tibbles turned his energies to the plight of the western farmer, in 1892 publishing a Populist tract, *The American Peasant*. He left Omaha the next year to become a reporter for a Farmers' Alliance syndicate and in 1895 founded the *Independent*, the official publication of the Populist party, in Lincoln, Nebraska. In a final show of reformist enthusiasm he ran for vice-president on the 1904 Populist ticket. Bright Eyes died in 1903, and Tibbles remarried four years later. He remained in Lincoln, first editing the weekly *Investigator* and then writing for the *Omaha World-Herald* almost until his death in 1928.

Standing Bear, the Ponca chief whose fate had once engrossed Tibbles and a corps of other sincere and well-intentioned reformers, stayed on the Dakota reservation and took land there when allotments were finally made in 1890. The old chief's name crops up again in government reports for that year. He had temporarily moved his band down to the Indian Territory reservation to be among his relatives. Although he soon returned, the Ponca agent and the missionary-schoolteacher thought he had disrupted the tribe's progress and considered him a reactionary element.[14]

13. Tibbles, *Buckskin and Blanket Days*, p. 316.
14. *Fifty-Ninth Report of the Commissioner of Indian Affairs* (Washington: G.P.O., 1890), pp. 146–47.
    Just slightly more than a fourth of the tribe—approximately 225 out of about 825—had elected to stay in Dakota when allotments were made (Frederick Webb Hodge, ed., *Handbook of American Indians North of Mexico*, Bulletin 30 of the Bureau of American Ethnology [1906; reprinted New York: Pageant, 1959], pt. 2, p. 279).

(Similar complaints about "retrograde" leaders were voiced at agencies throughout the West as it became apparent that even those Indians who seemed most willing to accommodate to white culture were not about to give up all their traditional practices.) Standing Bear died in obscurity in 1908. He and many of his counterparts in other tribes never did adopt the white way of life exactly as the humanitarians had envisioned. Yet by their alliance in the battle for Indian rights, Standing Bear and the reformers had brought all native Americans a step closer to achieving justice.

Note on the Text

The Ponca Chiefs was first published in Boston in 1880 as part of the national campaign for reform in Indian policy. Tibbles's personal copy of the book, which was presented to the Nebraska State Historical Society by his widow, carries on the copyright page the handwritten notation "This book was compiled from extracts made from reportorial notes in the Omaha Herald, written when I was working sixteen hours a day and published without revision or even seeing the proofs. T. H. Tibbles." It parallels very closely his newspaper stories from April 1 to May 20, 1879; many passages are copied verbatim. The front cover of the first edition—there were at least two—carries the price, fifty cents; and an announcement on the back tells us that "all the profits accruing from the sale of this book at public meetings, held in behalf of the Indians," were to be "devoted to securing, through the regular processes of the courts, the recovery of the lands taken by force from the Ponca Indians, and to settling the question, by a decision of the highest legal tribunal of the country, whether the life and property of an Indian can be protected by law." On the inside front and back covers are resolutions by Boston Philanthropic groups supporting the Ponca cause and the reform program advocated by the humanitarians and Secretary Schurz.

This edition reprints the text of the first edition exactly, with the following exceptions: the subtitle "An Account of the Trial of Standing Bear" has been added; the title page carries Tibbles's name rather than the pseudonym Zylyff; obvious typographical errors have been corrected silently; several footnotes have been supplied; and the wording of the petition and return (pp. 36–45) has been brought into conformity with that of the records in the district court file on the case. All of the discrepancies in the documents were minor, most involving either a miscopying of single words—"were" for "was," "there" for "then," etc.—or the omission of words or short phrases. The *Ponca Chiefs* version of the legal papers also differs somewhat from the original in punctuation and paragraphing, but in no instance is the meaning affected. Footnotes added in this edition are bracketed and labeled *ed. note.*

The accuracy of the book is difficult to assess with much assurance: not only is it necessary to allow for Tibbles's obvious bias, but there is little to test his account against. Other newspapers seem to have relied heavily on Tibbles's dispatches, and the section dealing in greatest detail with the Ponca controversy is missing from the John G. Bourke diary, the only other known eyewitness account. However, in his description of Crook's March 31 interview with Standing Bear, Bourke includes Tibbles's report from the next day's *Daily Herald* (pp. 29–32) and calls it accurate.[1] Furthermore, it seems significant that the district court

1. Bourke, "Conference held between Brigadier General George Crook and a small band of Indians of the Ponca Tribe," Bourke Diary.

file on the case includes Tibbles's transcription of Judge
Dundy's opinion from the May 13 *Daily Herald* (Chapter
X) in lieu of any other version of the decision. The only
specific point on which there is any discrepancy between
the newspaper stories and *The Ponca Chiefs* is the date of
the hearing. While the book says the trial started on April
30, both the *Omaha Daily Herald* and the *Lincoln Daily
State Journal* clearly indicate that formal proceedings
opened on May 1. The May 1 *Daily Herald* does suggest,
however, that there was an informal session on the evening
of April 30. Details of the Poncas' removal and experience
in Indian Territory up to the time of Standing Bear's flight
do not jibe exactly with government reports, but the in-
consistencies only point up the extreme difficulty, later
noted by the senatorial committee investigating the case,
of conducting relations with a tribe through interpreters
who often could not convey each side's intentions accur-
ately and who frequently themselves did not understand
the points at issue.

A comparison of Tibbles's three versions of the affair—
in the *Daily Herald*, *The Ponca Chiefs*, and his autobiography, *Buckskin and Blanket Days*—shows that he did
embellish some of the more dramatic incidents in later re-
tellings. The newspaper accounts do not mention the "skin
of a different hue" passage alluded to in Standing Bear's
address to the court (this speech is much embroidered in
Buckskin and Blanket Days), nor does the *Daily Herald*'s
description of Standing Bear's farewell to Webster include
the "I have found a better way" passage. While this does
not mean that Tibbles invented Standing Bear's orations,
it does suggest that he elaborated on them. An example
of Tibbles's tendency to indulge his readers' taste for melo-

drama is seen in the account of Standing Bear's courtroom speech in *Buckskin and Blanket Days*, which is farthest removed from the events (it was written in 1905) and is probably the least accurate of the three versions. The circumstances of the address are passed over in *The Ponca Chiefs*, but in his later book Tibbles describes them thus:

When the attorneys had ended their arguments, Judge Dundy announced that he would hand down his decision later. . . . All eyes were fixed on the sad, mild, yet strong face of Standing Bear, who sat in front of the judge. And only the two or three persons nearest the bench heard an interesting bit of routine.

For the marshal came close to Judge Dundy, who murmured to him, "Court is adjourned."

The marshal, carefully facing front, proclaimed even more softly, "Hear ye! The Honorable District Court of the United States is now adjourned."

Then Judge Dundy told Standing Bear that he might speak; and neither the chief nor the audience dreamed that the court session already was officially over.[2]

Yet it is apparent from the May 4 and May 6 *Daily Herald*s that Standing Bear's address was not preceded by such an episode and that the lawyers knew in advance that he would be allowed to speak.

The two books also differ on just how Tibbles came to be involved in the Ponca situation to begin with. In *Buckskin and Blanket Days* he says that General Crook came to see him in the *Daily Herald* editorial rooms and asked him to help the Poncas. This could be true. The autobiography was written after Crook's death, when Tibbles would have felt no need to protect the general; and one authority on Crook thinks that although Tibbles may have invented

2. Tibbles, *Buckskin and Blanket Days*, p. 200.

the dialogue between the two men, the action would have been in character for Crook.[3]

In sum, *The Ponca Chiefs*, taken in conjunction with the *Daily Herald* stories, is probably as accurate an account of the basic facts of the court case as we are likely to get. And the book as a whole is indisputably true to the spirit of the reformist milieu in which it was written.

3. King, "'A Better Way,'" p. 244.

Acknowledgments

The University of Nebraska Press wishes to express its gratitude to Miss Esther Montgomery, staff writer of the Nebraska ETV Network, who first proposed this publishing project and undertook much of the original research upon which the editor drew. We also wish to thank James T. King, professor of history, University of Wisconsin, River Falls, who provided valuable leads to sources of information on the Standing Bear case and offered many helpful suggestions on the manuscript.